NEW BREAKTHROUGH PRAYERS

(For Victory and Abundant Blessings in all life's situations)

Peter O. ADENMOSUN

New Breakthrough Prayers — For Victory and Abundant Blessings in all life's situations

Copyright ©
Reverend Peter O. ADENMOSUN
CHRTOGM Ministry

New Breakthrough Prayers

Reprinted, **2015**

All rights reserved:
No portion of this book may be reproduced, stored in a retrieval system, or transmitted in any form or by any means, electronic, mechanical, electrostatic, magnetic tape, photocopying, recording or otherwise, without the prior written permission of the copyright owner.
Scripture quotations marked (AMP) have been taken from the Amplified Bible.
Scripture quotations marked (KJV) have been taken from the King James Version.
Scripture quotations marked (NKJV) have been taken from the New King James Version.

ISBN: 978-1-32624300-5

For Prayer and Counseling, Please Contact:

Nigeria:
Christ Total Gospel Ministries International
Amazing Grace Haven
Off Obasanjo way, Ita-Iyalode
P.O. Box 2145, Sapon, Abeokuta
Ogun State. Nigeria
Tel: +234803 329 7495

United Kingdom:
Tel: +447951101349, +447769890144, +447961075197
E-mail: chrtogm@gmail.com
Website: www.chrtogm.org
Facebook: Chrtogm Media Outreach;
Twitter: Chrtogm

Available to order from:
www.lulu.com; www.amazon.co.uk;
www.amazon.com;
other amazon sites and various online stores

Design & Printed in Nigeria by:
vicadex® PRINT MEDIA
+2348101111139, +2348079727187

* For Victory and Abundant Blessings in all life's situations

CONTENTS

CONTENTS		
DEDICATION		iii
ACKNOWLEDGMENT		v
FOREWORD		vi
PREFACE		vii
INTRODUCTION		viii
CHAPTER 1:	PRAYER OF PRAISE AND THANKSGIVING	01
CHAPTER 2:	PRAISE UNTO OUR GOD ALMIGHTY	06
CHAPTER 3:	PRAYER OF FORGIVENESS AND REPENTANCE	07
CHAPTER 4:	DIFFERENT LIFE'S BATTLES THAT CONFRONTS PEOPLE	11
CHAPTER 5:	DAILY PRAYERS FOR GOD'S SPECIAL INTERVENTION IN ALL MATTERS	12
CHAPTER 6:	AFTER A BAD DREAM	16
CHAPTER 7:	PRAYER OF VICTORY OVER DIVERSE BATTLES	18
CHAPTER 8:	PRAYER FOR JOURNEY MERCIES	21
CHAPTER 9:	VICTORY OVER HOUSEHOLD AND NEIGHBORHOOD ENEMIES	23
CHAPTER 10:	PRAYER FOR VICTORY WHEN A WOMAN SUFFERS MISCARRIAGES	26
CHAPTER 11:	VICTORY OVER DIFFERENT COVENANTS AND CURSES	28
CHAPTER 12:	PRAYER OF VICTORY OVER FEAR, DISMAY, TERROR AND CONFUSION OF MIND	30
CHAPTER 13:	PRAYER OF DELIVERANCE FROM FINANCIAL AFFLICTION	33
CHAPTER 14:	INABILITY TO GET WEALTH	35
CHAPTER 15:	PRAYER AGAINST ANGER AND EVIL THOUGHTS	37
CHAPTER 16:	PRAYER AGAINST FAILURE AND DISAPPOINTMENT	39
CHAPTER 17:	DEBT, DEVOURER, SALES BLOCKER AND ASSOCIATE PROBLEMS	41
CHAPTER 18:	PRAYER OF VICTORY OVER OBSTACLES AND OBSTRUCTIONS ON YOUR WAY	43
CHAPTER 19:	VICTORY OVER THE SPIRIT OF DEATH	45
CHAPTER 20:	FAVOUR OF GOD IN EVERY WAY	47
CHAPTER 21:	VICTORY OVER BARRENNESS	49
CHAPTER 22:	OVERCOMING LONG-STANDING PROBLEMS	51
CHAPTER 23:	ENEMY WHO PURSUES RELENTLESSLY	53
CHAPTER 24:	PRAYERS TO CONFRONT EVERY POWER OF THE ENEMY OVER YOUR WORK	55
CHAPTER 25:	PRAYER OVER DIFFERENT BATTLES OF THE ENEMY IN ONE'S LIFE	57
CHAPTER 26:	PRAYER FOR PREGNANT WOMEN	59
		61

CHAPTER 27:	WHEN YOUR SPOUSE IS UNFAITHFUL AND TROUBLESOME	63
CHAPTER 28:	PRAYER FOR ALL STUDENTS AND THOSE GOING FOR INTERVIEW OR EXAMINATION	65
CHAPTER 29:	FOR ALL CONTRACTORS	68
CHAPTER 30:	FOR THOSE LOOKING UNTO GOD FOR MARITAL PARTNERS	70
CHAPTER 31:	WHEN YOUR CHILD IS STUBBORN AND DISOBEDIENT	72
CHAPTER 32:	VICTORY OVER GETTING ROBED IN ANOTHER MAN'S CRIME, RUNNING INTO TROUBLE OF CASE	74
CHAPTER 33:	PRAYER OF VICTORY OVER FLESH	76
CHAPTER 34:	PERSONAL DELIVERANCE	78
CHAPTER 35:	WAGING WAR AGAINST SEPARATION AND DIVORCE IN MARRIAGE	81
CHAPTER 36:	PRAYER FOR SPECIAL GOODNESS	83
CHAPTER 37:	VICTORY OVER ALL SPIRITS OF IMPOSSIBILITY	85
CHAPTER 38:	SUNDAY, SUNDAY PRAYER TABLETS	86
CHAPTER 39:	VICTORY OVER DIVERSE DISEASES AND SICKNESS	88
CHAPTER 40:	PRAYER OF DELIVERANCE FROM ALL AFFLICTIONS	90
CHAPTER 41:	DAILY PRAYERS ON OPEN DOORS FOR DIVINE BLESSINGS	92
CHAPTER 42:	PRAYER FOR HELP FROM ALL WAYS FOR YOUR BUSINESS OR WORK	94
CHAPTER 43:	DAILY DEMANDING FOR ONE'S RIGHTS	96
CHAPTER 44:	SPECIAL PRAYER ON TORMENTORS	98
CHAPTER 45:	PRAYER FOR GOD'S GENERAL PROTECTION	99
CHAPTER 46:	GENERAL PURPOSE PRAYER POINTS FOR TOTAL RECOVERY	101
CHAPTER 47:	PRAYER FOR THE BEREAVED	106
CHAPTER 48:	PRAYER FOR LONGEVITY	108
CHAPTER 49:	BLESSING ON A NEWLY BUILT, BOUGHT, LEASED HOUSE OR LAND	110
CHAPTER 50:	BLESSING FOR NEWLY MARRIED COUPLE	112
CHAPTER 51:	BLESSING FOR A NEW BORN BABY	114
CHAPTER 52:	PRAYER FOR THOSE CELEBRATING THEIR BIRTHDAY	116
CHAPTER 53:	DELIVERANCE PRAYER FOR HANDS	118
CHAPTER 54:	DELIVERANCE PRAYER FOR LEGS OR FEET UNDER ATTACK	121
CHAPTER 55:	DELIVERANCE PRAYERS FOR HEADS UNDER ATTACK	123
CHAPTER 56:	DELIVERANCE PRAYERS FOR LANDS UNDER ATTACK	126
CHAPTER 57:	DELIVERANCE PRAYERS FROM DEMONIC ATTACK OF SPIRITUAL COBWEB	130
CHAPTER 58:	DELIVERANCE PRAYERS FROM POVERTY	132
CHAPTER 59:	DELIVERANCE PRAYERS FOR THE FIRSTBORN	134
CHAPTER 60:	DELIVERING YOUR POSITIVE DESTINY THROUGH ONE HUNDRED PRAYER QUAKES	137

HOW TO ADMINISTER A PERSONAL DELIVERANCE   144

BEGINNING A RELATIONSHIP WITH JESUS CHRIST   146

SCRIPTURE GUIDE   148

DEDICATION

First and foremost I would like to dedicate this book to *my Creator, God the Father, Jesus Christ my Lord and personal Saviour* and the Holy Spirit who gave me the vision and strength to write bring out this book.

This book is dedicated to **Pastors Daniel and Sade Olukoya** of *Mountain of Fire and Miracles Ministries* whose prayer's life and ministry have help me a lot in my ministerial life,

To my brothers and sisters *Mr and Mrs Dayo Salako and Evangelist and Mrs Femi Okunade* for their contributions in our ministry and the printing of this prayer book.

To all Prayer Team all over the world who are sincerely praying.

To all those that will use this book for prayer to receive their miracles

For Victory and Abundant Blessings in all life's situations

ACKNOWLEDGMENT

First and foremost I would like to give thanks to my Creator, God the Father, Jesus Christ my Lord and personal Saviour and the Holy Spirit who opened my eyes to see and sustained me to write this book.

My beloved co-workers in *Christ Total Gospel Ministries International* all over the world.

My profound thanks goes to *my wife,* Oluyemisi Adenike Adenmosun, my only portion, and my begotten son Iyanu Jesujuwon Adenmosun for believing in me and encouraging me by giving me all necessary supports always.

I also want to appreciate every one committed to the printing and distribution of this book worldwide, all members of the *All Nations for Christ Baptist Church* and everyone that has made the vision of *Christ Total Gospel Ministries International* a reality. God bless you all. Amen.

FOREWORD

Prayer changes things, circumstances, people, nations and destinies of men. There is no limit to what can be achieved if only we pray, as we ought to. The great and mighty things, which God wants us to achieve on earth and bless us with, are limited by the inadequacies of our prayers and how to approach the situation in prayer. Therefore, this prayer book will serve as inspiration to many who are looking forward to breakthrough in prayer for their lives situation. To many Christians, prayer is like a mountain they find very difficult to climb. For such people, this book will be very useful to get them started as they embrace dynamic prayer life, and it will also assist them to overcome their *"prayer mountains and difficulties"*. They will be on their own in the exciting realm of dynamic and consistent prayer life. It is really wonderful and exciting to have a habit of consistent and vibrant prayer life and to know when to pray, how to pray and what type of prayer to pray. I respect and commend the great compassion for souls of men and those oppressed by the devil, which has inspired **Evangelist Peter O. Adenmosun** to write this book. I also commend the effort and zeal put into writing this book. I pray the purpose of the book shall be achieved, and also that this prayer book will bring forth: breakthrough, victories and testimonies that will last for eternity in the lives of all who will use it, in Jesus' name *(Amen)*.

- Pastor Kola Alabi

PREFACE

All glory to God the Father, Jesus the Son and the Holy Spirit who is our Comforter, the Three-in-One God who has made it possible for me to make a compilation and publication of this book at this time. Glory be to God on high *(Amen)*. This book is the revelation and publication of what God has put in our mind at the Christ Total Gospel Ministries International, for the deliverance of the creatures of God whom Satan is torturing. This book is a guide to prayers that are in line with the word of God. It is not a book of magic, and should not be view or taken as one. My people, it is a great privilege to be a man or woman of prayer! Therefore, use this opportunity before it is too late. *"Pray that you may not pray"*. If you can indeed use this book with faith and confidence in God, it shall be a great gain for you *(Heb. 11:1)*. When it comes to prayer, after your Bible, take this book as highly important; buy copies as gifts to bless others. Make it your companion, for it will surely help you. This book will do three major things in your life: *firstly,* it will enable you to know many prayer points. *Secondly,* it will help you to pray and prevent you from praying amiss. *Thirdly,* it will bring victory and solution to your situation in life as you apply the instructions in it, in your prayers. The peace of God is yours, in Jesus' name *(Amen)*.

- **Rev. Peter O. Adenmosun**

• For Victory and Abundant Blessings in all life's situations

INTRODUCTION

We have suggested prayer points for you in this book. The prayer points will show you the way to victory over difficult life situations. They will also give you marvellous blessings in your work or business. Jesus asked Bartimeus, the blind *"What do you want me to do for you?"* Bartimeus answered, *"That I may see"*. Do you really know what you want the Lord to do for you? Bartimeus knew what he wanted. You too should know what you want from the Lord.

To use this book, therefore,
1. Decide to pray and prepare yourself very well for prayer. Remember, prayer is talking with one's creator. Ask the Lord to help you not to pray amiss.
2. Find an appropriate time and the right place where you can pray without disturbance. You can use this book when you are alone.
3. Open to the right prayer(s) that you need and are relevant to your situation and confront your problems in prayer with confidence and faith.
4. You may as well use the prayer points during your family altars, church worship sessions, prayer vigils or at prayer meetings, either in the morning or afternoon. Fasting could also be involved if you so desired. It will help you to have self-control, and gives you full concentration while praying.
5. Believe that your prayers will be answered, and so shall it be, in Jesus' name.

ABOUT FASTING

Fasting is highly important in prayer and that is why I think you should fast to support these prayers, if you are in good condition of health to do so. Fasting is denying oneself of the things one loves to do every day in order to seek the face of the Living God. For instance, denying oneself of food, water, sleep, sex with one's partner, and so on.

DURATION OF FASTING

The numbers of the days of fasting mentioned in the Bible vary, but the followings were recorded in the scriptures. They are still useful and practicable today depending on the leading of the Holy Spirit.

* 1 day   —   *Daniel 9:23, 20-27, Judges 20:26ff*
* 3 days   —   *Esther 4:13 –16, 5:1-9*
* 7 days   —   *II Sam. 12:16 –32, I Sam. 31:13*
* 14 days   —   *Acts 27:33 –34*
* 21 days   —   *Daniel 10: 3 –13*
* 40 days   —   *Deut. 9:9; 25 –29; 10:10; I Kings 19:7–18, Matt. 4:1-11*

SOME EARLY PEOPLE WHO FASTED IN THE BIBLE
1. The children of Israel fasted – *Esther 4:16*.
2. The disciples including Paul fasted – *Acts 13:1-3, 14:21-23, Luke. 4:1-23, – II Cor.5, Acts 9:9*.
3. Jesus fasted – *Matthew 4:11, 6:16 and 17:21, Mark 2:18-20*.
4. God wants us to fast– *Joel 1:13–18, Jonah 3:1-10*.

BENEFITS OF FASTING
1. It makes the spiritual realm easily accessible.
2. It generates holy boldness.
3. It helps our obedience to God.
4. It makes the devil to flee when believers pray.
5. It helps in receiving better revelations.
6. It subdues the flesh and helps our spirits to receive quick revelations from above.

TYPES OF FASTING
1. **Dry Fasting/Marathon:** This is a total abstinence from food for a specific period. It is also called absolute fasting *(Acts 9:9.)* It is Marathon when it continues without you breaking it at the end of the day.

2. **Normal Fasting:** The fast that ends every evening at 6p.m (Normal).
3. **Partial Fasting:** During partial fasting, light meals and drink are eaten. This type of fast is done mostly by sick people or pregnant women.

WHEN DO YOU NEED TO FAST?
1. When you need to have deeper spiritual experience.
2. When a problem confronts you.
3. When you need to make a serious confession.
4. When you want to make a powerful decision.
5. When you need spiritual renewal.
6. When one has strayed away in the spirit and so on.

PRECAUTIONS BEFORE, DURING AND AFTER FASTING
1. The heart must be cleansed and sanctified.
2. Give yourself to the word of God and to prayer.
3. Have specific goal for the fast.
4. Do not announce your fast like some people do.
5. Avoid unnecessary movements and talking around.
6. Do not relent as you embark on long fasting.
7. Do not use heavy meal to break a long fasting
8. Avoid rushing to eat heavy food after you have broken your fast.

THE THOUGHT OF GOD FOR YOUR SALVATION
Many people today want quick answers to their prayers and this is normal and possible if we can examine ourselves and take the correct steps *(2 Cor. 13:5)*. The word of God says, *"We cannot abide in sin and expect grace to increase"*. Our Creator detests sin completely. There are numerous hindrances to getting answers to your prayers. These may be the sins we have refused to confess to God, unrepentant spirit, unbiblical approach to prayer, unforgiveness, stubbornness, quarrel between couple, impatience, insufficient praise to God and failure to thank the Creator appropriately. Unbelief and several other

For Victory and Abundant Blessings in all life's situations

shortcomings can also hinder your prayer. However, God has a plan for your life. Do you know the plan? Peace and eternal life for you. It is a divine favour. Accept it today. Listen, if you are brought before God now, and you are asked to state whether or not you are guilty for the way you live presently, what will be your response? Remember the Bible says, *"For all have sinned and fall short of the glory of God" (Roman 6:23)*, what will you say or what shall your defence be before God. Therefore, accept the plan of God to save your soul today by accepting Jesus Christ as your Lord and Saviour. Doing this has to do with the kind of answer you will receive to your prayers. The problem of sin in your life must be dealt with in order for you to receive special blessings from God. Friend, there is great news for you:

THE CONDEMNATION OF MAN
- He that fails to accept Jesus as Saviour and Lord shall forfeit the glory or favour of God:
- For all have sinned and fall short of the glory of God – Romans 3:23.

THE CALL OF GOD
God is calling daily; hear what He says in His word:
"Come now, and let us reason together, says the Lord: though your sins be as scarlet, they shall be as white as snow, though they be red like crimson, they shall be white as wool"

Isaiah 1:18

GOD MADE AN EXCHANGE WITH HIS SON
God, who did not want us to die and be condemned eternally, gave His Son Jesus Christ to die in our place, so that we may have eternal life:
"...but the gift of God is eternal life through Jesus Christ our Lord.
Romans 6:23

"Who his own self bare our sins in his own body on the tree, that we, being dead to sins, should live unto righteousness by whose stripes ye were healed"

I Peter 2:24.

- For Victory and Abundant Blessings in all life's situations

SALVATION
Accepting Jesus Christ is a simple thing you have to do:
Therefore, repent and believe the gospel, Verbally confess the Lord Jesus as your Lord and Saviour, believe with all your heart that God raised Him from the dead, and you shall be saved *Romans 10:9-10; Mark 1:15*.

All these rumours of wars economic hardship and increase in wickedness and other evil deeds around us are calling our attention to the fact that the Second Coming of Jesus is near. Beloved, be prepared. It is about time to go home. Jesus Christ is about returning. Flee from sin; be holy in thoughts, attitudes and deeds – *Rom. 12:1-2*. This is because holy and perfect is our God. You are blessed as you expect the return of Jesus Christ – *1 Peter 2:24*. You too can be a soul winner today by telling somebody about the love of Christ. That is God's will for you.

ADVANTAGES OF SOUL-WINNING
1. It affords you an opportunity of been a blessing to other people, making new friends everyday and sharing the love of Christ with someone.
2. It places you in the position to be blessed of God.
3. It helps you to enjoy the joy that obedience brings.
4. It brings refreshment from the Lord.
5. It keeps you busy for the Lord.
6. It gives you the joy of knowing that a soul won through you is saved from eternal damnation.
7. It helps you to maintain a link with God.
8. It helps you to live a holy life.
9. It promotes a prayerful life.
10. It gives you eternal reward.
11. It gives you the opportunity of working and walking with God.

Chapter 1

PRAYER OF PRAISE AND THANKSGIVING

Read: *II Sam. 22:4, Ps. 147:1, Ps. 50:23; Ps. 47:1, 6, 7;*
Ps. 48:1; 63:3-5; 92:1; 107:8; Acts 16:25, Eph. 5:18-20,
Deut. 28:46 – 47 Ps. 100:1-4.

Sing: ** All hail the power of Jesus name...*
* To God be the glory...

(Sing other praise songs that you know very well. If you can praise God in the spirit, do it because it is very good.)

1. **Praise God for:**
   * His goodness.
   * His greatness.
   * His wonderful works unto man.
   * He is the King of the whole earth.
   * He created all things
   * His holiness.
   * His mercy and His protection.
   * His knowledge, understanding and wisdom.

2. **Thank Him for:**
   * All He had done.
   * What He is doing presently.
   * What He will do today.
   * Your creation, salvation, family, work, healing, blessing and so on.

It is good to praise God and thank Him— *Ps. 100:1, 4;* Begin to call His names, praise Him with songs of praise and thanksgiving, and it shall be well with you.

Sing: ** I will sing of the mercies of the Lord forever...*
* His name is higher...
* Majesty, worship His majesty...

• For Victory and Abundant Blessings in all life's situations

SALVATION
Accepting Jesus Christ is a simple thing you have to do:
Therefore, repent and believe the gospel, Verbally confess the Lord Jesus as your Lord and Saviour, believe with all your heart that God raised Him from the dead, and you shall be saved *Romans 10:9-10; Mark 1:15.*

All these rumours of wars economic hardship and increase in wickedness and other evil deeds around us are calling our attention to the fact that the Second Coming of Jesus is near. Beloved, be prepared. It is about time to go home. Jesus Christ is about returning. Flee from sin; be holy in thoughts, attitudes and deeds – *Rom. 12:1-2.* This is because holy and perfect is our God. You are blessed as you expect the return of Jesus Christ – *1 Peter 2:24.* You too can be a soul winner today by telling somebody about the love of Christ. That is God's will for you.

ADVANTAGES OF SOUL-WINNING
1. It affords you an opportunity of been a blessing to other people, making new friends everyday and sharing the love of Christ with someone.
2. It places you in the position to be blessed of God.
3. It helps you to enjoy the joy that obedience brings.
4. It brings refreshment from the Lord.
5. It keeps you busy for the Lord.
6. It gives you the joy of knowing that a soul won through you is saved from eternal damnation.
7. It helps you to maintain a link with God.
8. It helps you to live a holy life.
9. It promotes a prayerful life.
10. It gives you eternal reward.
11. It gives you the opportunity of working and walking with God.

Chapter 1

PRAYER OF PRAISE AND THANKSGIVING

Read: II Sam. 22:4, Ps. 147:1, Ps. 50:23; Ps. 47:1, 6, 7;
Ps. 48:1; 63:3-5; 92:1; 107:8; Acts 16:25, Eph. 5:18-20,
Deut. 28:46 – 47 Ps. 100:1-4.

Sing: *All hail the power of Jesus name...*
To God be the glory...

(Sing other praise songs that you know very well. If you can praise God in the spirit, do it because it is very good.)

1. **Praise God for:**
   * His goodness.
   * His greatness.
   * His wonderful works unto man.
   * He is the King of the whole earth.
   * He created all things
   * His holiness.
   * His mercy and His protection.
   * His knowledge, understanding and wisdom.

2. **Thank Him for:**
   * All He had done.
   * What He is doing presently.
   * What He will do today.
   * Your creation, salvation, family, work, healing, blessing and so on.

It is good to praise God and thank Him– Ps. 100:1, 4; Begin to call His names, praise Him with songs of praise and thanksgiving, and it shall be well with you.

Sing: *I will sing of the mercies of the Lord forever...*
His name is higher...
Majesty, worship His majesty...

Chapter 2

PRAISE UNTO OUR GOD ALMIGHTY

Read: Ps 100: 1, Ps 96, I Sam 2
Sing: * *O Lord my God...*
       * *You are the Lord...*
(Sing these songs or others that the Lord may put in your mind. Your songs of praise to God will help in letting Him hear you properly.)

PRAYER OF PRAISE:

I adore the creator of the earth and the heaven, the powerful changer that changes times and seasons, the King that transforms one's portion and destiny, the King that renews one's life, the King that gives, plants and harvests. The King that is firmly established, God of gods, King of kings, and the King that created the whole earth. No one will ever know how you came into being. You are the King who knows where the world originated from, but no one knows your origin. You are the King that no one dare question. You are my God that is called the Almighty, the Father of the entire world. You are unquestionable King of kings, who appointed the sun to reign in the day and the moon and stars to reign at night; the King that does, as He desires. You are the mighty King that destroys the power of death and diseases. You are the King that shatters coffins and cancels cases. You are the Lord, my Father, my Rock, my Resting Place, my Head, my Song, my Victory, my Life and my God. You are all in all for me. Thank you!

Sing: I have a Father...

God, you are the head of the whole world; you are King of kings, my own God, my own Father, my own Master, my own Power, my own

| 07 |

Lover, my own Rock, my own Song and the Head of the universe. I fear you, my own God, I worship you. You are the King that answers by fire; you are the Head of the world, the one with uncountable names. Your name is more efficacious than herbs and charms. You are the one whose praises we cannot exhaust, the Almighty and my own king.

Sing: You are the Lord...

God of love, you are the unquestionable Almighty with the garment of fire, with the undergarment of sun, the indomitable sovereign in the heavens. You are the King that sends winds on errands, the King that rides on the back of storms, the advocate behind the orphans, the Saviour we can run to. You are the one who stands steadfastly behind the righteous —— Emmanuel. The one who goes about doing good, the Root of the house of Jesse, the King that sits enthroned in the temple and His train and kingly robes fill the temple. You are the eternal Rock, the Lion of the tribe of Judah. Halleluyah to your majesty!

Sing: O! That men will praise the Lord...

Then continue to praise Him:
Faithful Father, you are the exalted powerful one, the one that did wonders in the womb of a virgin. He established his glory in a woman. His influence is in the entire world. You are the Word that dwells and speaks within a man, the King that is immortal, that never fades and is indestructible. You are the Ancient One who never changes title, the King with mighty hand that rescues His children from the pit of the world. You are the King that fills the earth and the heavens, the King that never fails in His promises, the King who can do everything He says, I adore you. I adore you, the God of Abraham, the King that was, yesterday, the King that is, today, the King that will be forever. You are the King that decorates His body with crown and the hill of light. The King that shines like lighting in the sky, the unquestionable, the unchallengeable God. The one who knows Him does not meet Him;

For Victory and Abundant Blessings in all life's situations

the one who meets Him does not know Him, the King that has no competitor. I reverence you.

Sing: Oh! Lord, I am very, very grateful...

O! My Jesus, you are the First and the Last, the Beginning and the End! You are the keeper of creations and the Creator of all. You are the Architect of the universe and the Manager of all times. You were always, you are always, and you will always be. You are unmoved, unchanged and undefeatable Being. You were bruised but brought healing! You were pierced to ease our pains! You were persecuted but brought freedom! You were dead but brought life! You were raised and brought power! You reign to give us peace! The world cannot understand you; the military cannot defeat you, the schools cannot explain you and the leaders cannot ignore you, Herod could not kill you, the Pharisees could not confuse you, and the people could not hold you! Nero could not crush you, Hitler could not silence you, and the New Age cannot replace you! You are the light, my Love, and my Lord. You are good, kind and gentle. You are holy, righteous, mighty, powerful, and pure, your ways are right, your word is eternal, your will is unchanging, and your mind is on me.

Sing: His name is higher...

You are my Redeemer Jesus Christ, you are my Saviour, you are my guide, and you are my peace! You are my joy, you are my comfort, you are Lord, and you rule my life! I serve you because your bond is love, your burden is light, and your goal for me is abundant life. I follow you because you are the Wisdom of the wise, the Power of the powerful, the Ancient of days, the Ruler of rulers, the Leader of leaders, the Overseer of the overcomers, and the Sovereign Lord of all that was and is, and is to come. You will never leave me, never forsake me, never forget me, never mislead me, never overlook me, and never cancel my appointment in your appointment book! Whenever I fall, you lift me up!

Whenever I fail, you forgive! Whenever I am weak, you are strong! When I am lost, you are the way! Whenever I am afraid, you are my courage! Whenever I want to stumble, you keep me steady! Whenever I am hurt, you heal me! Whenever I am broken, you mend me! Whenever I am blind, you lead me! Whenever I am hungry, you feed me! Whenever I face trials, you are with me! Whenever I face problems, you comfort me! Whenever I face persecution, you shield me! Whenever I face losses, you provide for me! Whenever I face death, you carry me home! You are everything to everybody, everywhere, every time, and every way. You are God, you are faithful. I am yours, and you are mine! My Father in heaven can whip the father of this world. So, if people are wondering why I feel so secure, I understand this, that God is in control, I am on His side, and that means all is well with my soul.

Sing: * *Majesty, worship His majesty...*
   * *O Lord my God, when I in awesome wonder...*

Chapter 3

PRAYER OF FORGIVENESS AND REPENTANCE

Read: Ps. 51:1-3, 32; Job 11:13-16, Ps. 66:18; Mark 11:25-26; Pro. 28:13; I John 1:8-10, Ps. 57.

Sing: What can wash my sins away...

The word of God says, ***"For all have sinned and come short of the glory of God"*** *(Rom. 3:23).* This is the sin we inherited from Adam, our forefather. However, after you have accepted Jesus as your Saviour, if by accident you do wrong or slip into certain sins, if you ask for pardon, the Lord will forgive you. *(I John1:8-10).* It is a good thing to examine ourselves at all times and to confess our sins to our creator *(II Cor, 13:5)* so that sins will not constitute hindrances to our prayers *(Prov. 28:13).* Plead for forgiveness of all sins that you have committed that you can remember. The Spirit of God will remind you. Plead for the forgiveness of the sins of your family, town, country, and the whole world. Also, pray for forgiveness for the sins of unforgiveness, anger, envy, bitterness of heart, negative speech, lack of wisdom, disobedience unto God, bloodshed, backbiting, false witnessing and so on. Call the blood of Jesus several times to cleanse your entire life.

Read: I John 1:9; Is. 43:25; Jer. 31:34.

Receive your forgiveness with faith if you have truly confessed your sins *(Mk.11: 24).* Decide that you will not go back to them again.

Chapter 4

DIFFERENT LIFE'S BATTLES THAT CONFRONTS PEOPLE

Read: *John 16:33, Rev. 12:11*
Sing: ** When I survey the wondrous cross...*
   * Arise O Lord! and let your enemies be scattered...

The enemy confronts people with different and diverse battles in the world. Only God through Jesus Christ can save us. The death and resurrection of Jesus has established our victory by the blood He shed, through which He conquered Satan. *(Rev.12: 11)*. If any of the under listed battles is confronting your life, go to the Lord in prayer for victory over the battle.

Some of the battles always wage by the enemy are:
1. The battle that is difficult to fight.
2. The enemy we cannot but consult.
3. The enemy that creates problems for one.
4. Obstacles, Hindrances.
5. The enemy that follows one like a shadow.
6. The battle caused by oneself *(self-imposed)*.
7. Discontentment.
8. Inherited battle.
9. Battle that sticks to one very closely.
10. Foundation of one's pregnancy.
11. Enemy appointed by Satan to follow one around.
12. Cutting oneself out of measure.
13. Foundational— arising from the person that first lifted one on the day of birth.
14. Enemy that speaks evil of you.
15. Everyday battle.
16. Weekly battle.

- For Victory and Abundant Blessings in all life's situations

17. Monthly battle.
18. Yearly battle.
19. Negative utterance from one's parent (curse).
20. Enemy that jokes with you but destroys.
21. Enemy who knows you totally and does evil against you.
22. Enemies who do not know you but are on a mission to hurt you via demonic remote controls.
23. Enemy that harms and sympathises with you.
24. Relentless pursuer.
25. Enemy that shares your profits with you.
26. Enemy that enslaves one.
27. Enemy that inherits you along with your inheritance.
28. Enemy that follows one to the matrimonial home.
29. Enemy that waits for one in the matrimonial home.
30. Evil dreams.
31. Enemy that covers one's glory.
32. Rebellion *(in the family, at work, neighbourhood)*.
33. Enemy that hurts to death.
34. Life and property destroyer.
35. Enemy who exchanges one's goodness with evil.
36. Evil thoughts.
37. Irregular menstruation.
38. Tormentor.
39. Enemy that perches on you.
40. Contractors *(herbalists, false prophets and fake priests)*.
41. Co-operative enemies.
42. Debt.
43. The one who does good for you and yet does not make proper release.
44. Battle that wants to disgrace you.
45. Spiritual insects that are pest to your life.
46. Enemy that troubles you around.
47. Charms.
48. Enemy that kills that he may enjoy life.

49. Enemy that causes dismay.
50. Periodic battles.
51. Enemy that gently and gradually destroys one's life or property.
52. Enemy that makes you only to destroy you.
53. Wasters.
54. Enemy that is resolute to go any length to accomplish his evil wishes.
55. Battle that is designed to cause misfortune in one's business or employment.
56. Enemy that slides one backwards.
57. Enemy that prices you *(the herbalists, soothsayers or diviners)*.
58. Enemy that spiritually dictates limits to your profits in business and success in life.
59. Enemy that uses deception to rid one of one's blessing.
60. Enemy that turns one into a mediocre.
61. Enemy that seeks for opportunity to kill.
62. Enemy that derails God's promises for one's betterment.
63. Enemy that you can neither run away from nor move near.
64. Battle that follows one into the world.
65. Battle you run into.
66. Sudden destruction.
67. Battle that stops one's goodness.
68. Battle that shatters one's hope.
69. Enemy that gets ahead of you to your source of goodness.
70. Enemy that makes you stink to your benefactors.
71. Battle that places embargo on your progress.
72. Battle of "except"
73. Spell and trouble that are attached to a favour from unidentified enemy.
74. Battle that pins you to a corner.
75. Battle that reserves suffering for one.
76. Enemy that is close to you and hurts you.
77. Loss.
78. Enemy that ties one's goodness to a stake.

| 14 |

79. Battle that makes you a vagabond.
80. Enemy that sits on one's goodness.
81. Enemy that makes one regret one's life.
82. Enemy that ties one's goodness into the headgear or cap.
83. Enemy that changes one's goodness to sadness.

There are so many battles in life. Only Jesus can rescue one from them all. Therefore, the only antidote to the battles is for you to accept Jesus as your Lord and Saviour and your victory is sure. The Bible says, we overcame the dragon (devil) by the blood of the Lamb and the word of our testimony. Call on God through Jesus and it shall be well with you (Ps. 50:15, Jer. 33:3, Rev.21:12).

For Victory and Abundant Blessings in all life's situations

Chapter 5

DAILY PRAYERS FOR GOD'S SPECIAL INTERVENTION IN ALL MATTERS

Read: Ps. 136, 91, 121, 32:8, Isa. 30:21, Heb. 9:14, Jas. 1:5
Sing: * Holy, Holy, Holy, Holy, Holy is the Lord...
       * Majesty, worship His majesty...

God is always very eager to intervene in our situation if we will surrender and give Him a chance. So, you can ask Him today for divine intervention in your affairs. The Bible says, the hand of the Lord is not short that He cannot deliver; it is our sins that have made us far away from Him. Make-up your mind to serve and follow Him today, He will help you.

RAIN OF PRAYERS
1. Gracious God, put upon me today, the power to pray breakthrough prayers and the strength to travail in prayer as Jesus did at Gethsemane, in Jesus' name.
2. O Father, chase away all battles that might have followed me to this place of prayer. Deal with all of them with your mighty strength.
3. O God, fulfil the good covenants and plans that you have designed for me.
4. My life (three times), you must not react against prayer, in Jesus' name.
5. Lord, intervene in my matters. Let every area of my life be less refashioned by your divine power, in Jesus' name.
6. Anywhere the evil people have tied me to, Lord; set me loose today, in Jesus' name.
7. Today, my Lord, let me meet your divine favour and the goodwill of good people, in Jesus' name.
8. Holy Spirit, turn my life around and let it be great to your glory. As

• For Victory and Abundant Blessings in all life s situations

the rivulet finds its way to a river, let your goodness and mercy find me out today, in Jesus' name.

9. Holy Spirit, empower me today with the power that returns evil to the sender, in Jesus' name.

10. Lift up your two hands, call the name of Jesus seven times, and say: Holy Spirit, put on me, the power to suffer no more, in Jesus' name.

11. Holy Spirit put on me today the power that cannot be suppressed by the enemy, in Jesus' name.

12. Father, put on me the power to give birth to the good things in me for the world to see, all to your glory, in Jesus' name.

13. Lord, whatever or whoever is standing on my way to success and obstructing my progress, uproot and consume them with your fire, in Jesus' name.

14 My God, use your power to exalt me in every way this year, in Jesus' name.

15. Lord, pour down your rain of blessings on my business today, in Jesus' name.

16. My Creator, open the door to power for me today, in Jesus' name. Open for me, doors of help from the four corners of the world, in Jesus' name.

17. My Lord, let it be well with me today. Give me the strength to prosper. Open the door of big business for me today, in Jesus' name.

18. My God allow good things to happen in my life today, in Jesus' name.

19. My Lord, lead me to good things as I go out and come in today, in Jesus' name.

20. Raise help for me in a way that surpasses the knowledge of man; lead me to abundant blessings and miracles today, in Jesus' name.

Sing: *You are the Lord that is your name...*

Read: *Ps. 4; Mk. 6:46 – 47; Ps. 127:2; Pro. 3:32; Eccl. 15:12; Luke. 9:32; Ps. 24:16-17; Ps. 92: 1-2, 4-8.*

Chapter 6

AFTER A BAD DREAM

Sing: ** I plead the blood of Jesus...*
* Oh! The blood of Jesus...

There are different types of dreams, there are good and bad ones. It is possible for man to see the good, bad or dangerous things that are coming his way in his dream. If one is not careful, the enemy may take advantage of the bad dreams and use it to fight or attack one. They will not let one remember, so that one may not pray towards its fulfilment *(If it is good)* or against it *(If it is bad or evil)*. It can also be used to bring the spirit of fear into one's life for total destruction. Dream speaks of what has happened, what is happening presently or what is about to happen.

There are several demonic dreams e.g.:
1. Having sexual intercourse in one's dream
2. Eating in the dream.
3. Swimming in the river in the dream.
4. Being pursued by wild beasts: cow, snake and evil birds in the dream.
5. Seeing pepper in the dream.
6. Picking snails all around in the dream.
7. Being shot in the dream or drown in water
8. Gathering or carrying sticks.
9. Wearing ragged clothes.
10. Walking bare-footed.
11. Wearing shoes into wrong feet.
12. Missing a very important meeting
13. Coming late to the examination hall.

14. Picking unripe fruits.
15. Plucking decayed fruits.
16. Finding yourself in an uncompleted building.
17. Eating of the food placed before you by birds.
18. Falling down from high place.

If you suddenly find yourself unable to sleep, make sure you pray. It may be evil people holding a meeting on you somewhere at that time. If you are shown good things about your life in the dream, be careful of whom you tell. Remember Joseph in *Genesis 37:3–11*.

For comprehensive understanding on dream, inquire for our book on dream: You and Your Dreams, with over 150 interpretations.

THE RAIN OF PRAYERS
1. Use the prayer of praise and thanksgiving in this book to worship God.
2. Thank God for the miracles you have received from Him before.
3. Repent and ask for forgiveness of all the sins you have committed today.
4. All the pictures of evil dreams that Satan is bringing to me in my dreams, I reject them all and I say they are not mine, in Jesus' name.
5. Wherever the source of this evil vision is, let the fire of God scatter it, in Jesus' name.
6. All the weapons of evil dreams that the enemy is using on me, I completely consume them all with the fire of God, in Jesus' name.
7. I reject this evil dream, in Jesus' name *(Seven times)*.
8. I cover myself from the crown of my head to the soles of my feet with the blood of Jesus *(Seven times)*.
9. You angels of the Living God, surround this house now, in Jesus' name *(Three times)*.
10. Fire of God, I command you to start burning in this house now in the name of Jesus *(Seven times)*.

11. I remove every mark of evil dream from my life, in Jesus' name (Seven times).
12. I soak myself in the blood of Jesus.
13. I cover my bed, rooms, house and compound with the blood of Jesus.
14. Every sorrow that bad dreams had brought into my life, I cancel, in Jesus' name.
15. I deliver myself from every attack of bad dreams, in Jesus' name.
16. Father, put a total stop to bad dreams in my life, in Jesus' name.
17 My victory in Jesus is established and permanent, in Jesus' name.

Pray the prayer of deliverance in this book for yourself and your family before you sleep or after you have had bad dream. It is important.

Sing: Victory, victory hallelujah...

To overcome bad dreams in your life, you need to do the following things:

a. Give your life to Jesus as your Lord and Saviour.
b. Be filled with the power of Holy Ghost.
c. Live a clean and holy life.
d. Know and use the word of God.
e. be prayerful.
f. When you have any serious dream do not panic, only ask God for the meaning and the step He wants you to take.
g. You can seek the counsel of a genuine servant of God, either for counselling or deliverance.
h. You can write, phone or send e-mail to me through the address or numbers in the last page of this book.

- For Victory and Abundant Blessings in all life's situations

14. Picking unripe fruits.
15. Plucking decayed fruits.
16. Finding yourself in an uncompleted building.
17. Eating of the food placed before you by birds.
18. Falling down from high place.

If you suddenly find yourself unable to sleep, make sure you pray. It may be evil people holding a meeting on you somewhere at that time. If you are shown good things about your life in the dream, be careful of whom you tell. Remember Joseph in *Genesis 37:3–11*.

For comprehensive understanding on dream, inquire for our book on dream: You and Your Dreams, with over 150 interpretations.

THE RAIN OF PRAYERS

1. Use the prayer of praise and thanksgiving in this book to worship God.
2. Thank God for the miracles you have received from Him before.
3. Repent and ask for forgiveness of all the sins you have committed today.
4. All the pictures of evil dreams that Satan is bringing to me in my dreams, I reject them all and I say they are not mine, in Jesus' name.
5. Wherever the source of this evil vision is, let the fire of God scatter it, in Jesus' name.
6. All the weapons of evil dreams that the enemy is using on me, I completely consume them all with the fire of God, in Jesus' name.
7. I reject this evil dream, in Jesus' name *(Seven times)*.
8. I cover myself from the crown of my head to the soles of my feet with the blood of Jesus *(Seven times)*.
9. You angels of the Living God, surround this house now, in Jesus' name *(Three times)*.
10. Fire of God, I command you to start burning in this house now in the name of Jesus *(Seven times)*.

11. I remove every mark of evil dream from my life, in Jesus' name (Seven times).
12. I soak myself in the blood of Jesus.
13. I cover my bed, rooms, house and compound with the blood of Jesus.
14. Every sorrow that bad dreams had brought into my life, I cancel, in Jesus' name.
15. I deliver myself from every attack of bad dreams, in Jesus' name.
16. Father, put a total stop to bad dreams in my life, in Jesus' name.
17 My victory in Jesus is established and permanent, in Jesus' name.

Pray the prayer of deliverance in this book for yourself and your family before you sleep or after you have had bad dream. It is important.

Sing: Victory, victory hallelujah...

To overcome bad dreams in your life, you need to do the following things:
a. Give your life to Jesus as your Lord and Saviour.
b. Be filled with the power of Holy Ghost.
c. Live a clean and holy life.
d. Know and use the word of God.
e. be prayerful.
f. When you have any serious dream do not panic, only ask God for the meaning and the step He wants you to take.
g. You can seek the counsel of a genuine servant of God, either for counselling or deliverance.
h. You can write, phone or send e-mail to me through the address or numbers in the last page of this book.

For Victory and Abundant Blessings in all life s situations

Chapter 7

PRAYER OF VICTORY OVER DIVERSE BATTLES

Read: *Jn.16:33, Rev.12:11.*
Sing: ** Adonai, we worship you all my...*

Many are the afflictions of the righteous but the Lord delivers him from them all. When we face diverse battles, God has promised to be with us *(His children)* and gives us victory over them all. The weapon He has given unto us is prayer. He said. *"Ask, and it shall be given unto you"...* Ask now for victory on those diverse problems you are encountering. But are you righteous? Come to Jesus now He will do it and you will glorify Him.

THE RAIN OF PRAYERS

1. Lord, dash out the battle of my life to all my enemies today, in Jesus' name.
2. All battles arising from the *"curse of unless or except"* Lord, set them ablaze in my life, in Jesus' name.
3. For all that have planned to take away my life and that of my family this year, Lord, organise their destruction now, in Jesus' name.
4. All enemies who prevent me from growing according to the plan of God, Lord, cut them away, in Jesus' name.
5. All, who are waging war against me because of the glory of God upon my life, let them die, in Jesus' name.
6. All battles that are older than me and the ones I am older than, Lord, clear them away from my life, in Jesus' name.
7. All the mirrors, that the enemies are using to monitor my life around, Lord, let them be shattered into pieces today, in Jesus' name.
8. No matter how beautiful a shoe is, its face is always rubbed against

the ground, you host of heaven, begin to rub the faces of my enemies against the ground, in Jesus' name.
9. My Creator, all powers challenging you in my life, arise and answer them in your power, in Jesus' name.
10. All who want to usurp the glory of my life, if they fail to repent, heavenly Father, clear them away with sudden death, in Jesus' name.
11. All battles that entered my life when and where people are proud of me, host of heaven, begin to fight them, in Jesus' name.
12. Lord, all battles I brought upon myself at the time of ignorance roll them away, in Jesus' name.
13. Father, among those the power of the enemy will never harm, make me, my family and my business one, today, in Jesus' name.
14. All covenants the evil world has entered into with the sun, fire, rain, earth and wind over my life, my God, let them go back upon the lives of my enemies in Jesus' name.
15. All, who have been denying me meaningful life, Father, put them in jail, in Jesus' name.
16. Lord, use your storm of heaven to beat against the entire worldly storm fighting my life, in Jesus' name.
17. Lord, enough of battles in my life, give me rest in all areas, in Jesus' name.
18. The committee the enemy has set up to deliberate over the affairs of my life, Father, let them be swallowed up, in Jesus' name.
19. The hands of the clock never rest, all the enemies that say I will never rest, let restlessness and trouble enter their lives now, in Jesus' name.
20. Begin to send the fire of God into the camp of the enemy.
21. Cover yourself with the blood of Jesus.

Sing: Great is thy faithfulness...

For Victory and Abundant Blessings in all life's situations

Chapter 8

PRAYER FOR JOURNEY MERCIES

Read: Ps. 121: 2-3, Isa. 43:2-4, Ps. 118:12, Ex. 12:17, Ps. 24, 125:2, Heb. 1:14, Gen. 31:49, Ps. 121:1-7, Isa. 26:3
Sing: * Take control Holy Spirit...
* Rock of Ages cleft for me...

It is necessary for us most of the time to travel from one place to another. But a lot of people had travelled and never got to their destinations or got there, but never came back; due to one problem or the other on the road. The blood sucking demons always use this opportunity to destroy the lives of many people by making their vehicle or plane to crash or their ship to sink. I pray that this shall not be our portion in Jesus' name. Therefore, help yourself by praying.

Sing: Take control Holy Spirit...

THE RAIN OF PRAYERS
1   Thank God for protection that is certain through Jesus Christ over your journey.
2   Plead the blood of Jesus over yourself, the vehicle you are going to board, the driver and co-passengers. Let the blood of Jesus cleanse your way. Call the blood of Jesus for about a minute.
3   I nullify all the power and knowledge of the blood, sucking and destructive spirits over this journey in Jesus' name.
4   Holy Ghost fire and the shadow of the Almighty, envelope me throughout this journey in Jesus' name.
5   I came into this world in pool of blood, Lord, do not let me take my exit out of this world through pool of blood, I will not die through any accident, in Jesus' name.

For Victory and Abundant Blessings in all life's situations

6. Lord, the first thing I did when I was born was crying; do not let me cry in pain of accident out of this world, in Jesus' name.
7. In this journey, I shall not cause misfortune for anyone and nobody shall cause me misfortune, in Jesus' name.
8. All evil people as Achan in the house of Israel, O Lord! drive them away from this journey, in Jesus' name.
9. Holy Angels, surround me in this journey, in Jesus' name.
10. I confess that I shall not die a sudden death and I shall get to my destination, in Jesus' name.
11. I decree blindness upon the entire enemy assigned to follow me in this journey, in Jesus' name.
12. In Jesus name, I shall not have accident or delay, in this journey *(Seven times)*.
13. The mark of Jesus is on me; therefore, no one should trouble me in this journey, in Jesus' name *(Seven times)*.
14. With joy I board this vehicle and with joy I shall alight, in Jesus' name (Seven times).
15. The blood of Jesus is my protection and under this blood of the lamb, my protection is sure, in Jesus' name *(Seven times)*.
16. Yes, I shall glorify the Father at the end of this journey, in Jesus' name. *(Three times)*.
17. Plead the blood of Jesus on your (...)* for journey mercy from the Lord.
18. All powers that may want this (...)* to crash /sink I destroy your plans, in Jesus' name.
19. I destroy any covenant or appointment that anybody in this (...)* may have with death today, in Jesus' name.
20. O Lord! you are the God of journey in my life, grant me your safety today, in Jesus' name.
21. I mark the driver/sailor/pilot of this (...)* with the blood of Jesus, in Jesus' name.
22. All you blood sucking demons designated against this journey, I bind you and destroy your plans, in Jesus' name.

■ For Victory and Abundant Blessings in all life's situations

23. I confess that my blood shall not be shed by the enemy; I shall not become a victim of accident, in Jesus' name.
24. Let the angels of God, gather together to escort me on this journey, in Jesus' name.
25. I decree, that this journey shall be a blessing to me and all the people in this (...),* in Jesus' name.
26. The wind that is blowing this (...)* blow us to the coast of goodness and safety, in Jesus' name.
27. I remove the mark of death from every head in this (...)* by the blood of Jesus, in Jesus' name.

Begin to thank God, for giving you journey mercies. Praise Him with song of thanksgiving. Sing, pray and read the word of God into your heart as you travel. Meditate on the word and God will speak to you.

Sing: *I plead the blood the blood of Jesus...*
O Lord! I am very, very, grateful...

Name the mode of your transportation.

For Victory and Abundant Blessings in all life's situations

Chapter 9
VICTORY OVER HOUSEHOLD AND NEIGHBOURHOOD ENEMIES

Read: Matt. 10:36; Ps. 56:9; Gal. 6:17; Micah 7:6,
Isa. 8:9-10; 54: 15-17; Gen.37; Judges 15:9-13; Isa. 16:18,
Ex. 14:23 – 24; Gen. 11:7-8; Jer. 23:19.
Sing: * *It's not by power...*

Many times when we have problems we usually look outside our household and neighbourhood, but the Bible has confirmed it, that a man's household is his enemy. So, you have a battle to fight even within your household and neighbourhood. That problem you are having may not be from outside. Therefore, you need to pray.

THE RAIN OF PRAYERS
1. Plead the Blood of Jesus on your head for three minutes.
2. Lord, enlighten me that I may see where the enemy is hiding in my life, in Jesus' name.
3. Lord, confront my enemies from today and let there be no peace for their body and mind, in Jesus' name.
4. Today, I call the fire of Holy Ghost upon all household enemies troubling me; let the fire of God consume them completely, in Jesus' name.
5. Let all the power of my household enemies and their supporters be destroyed from today, in Jesus' name.
6. I confess that I am free from all the hands of all my enemies, in Jesus' name *(Seven times)*.
7. Let all my household enemies be troubled and confused over the affairs of my life, in Jesus' name *(Seven times)*.
8. All curses that have entered my life through the works of the enemies are totally destroyed by the blood of Jesus, in Jesus' name.

9. Lord, make me unapproachable and untouchable to my enemies, make me fire that cannot be handled by them, in Jesus' name.
10. Let the knowledge, preparedness and friendship among my enemies over the affairs of my life be scattered. Let confusion and misunderstanding be theirs from today, in Jesus' name.
11. I receive total deliverance out of the hands of all my enemies, in Jesus' name.
12. All the household and neighbourhood enemies like walls of Jericho in my life are swallowed up right now, in Jesus' name.
13. All co-operative enemies rebelling against me in the family and in my neighbourhood, according to the word of God, in Isaiah 8:9-10, be scattered, in Jesus' name.
14. All promise-diverting enemies battling me in the family and my neighbourhood, let the fire of God consume them all in Jesus' name.
15. My God, give to my enemies the troubles that they will be nurturing so much so that they will not remember to harm me again, in Jesus' name.
16 Thank God for your victory over the enemies. Praise Him with your whole heart.

Sing: *Jesus... your name is a miracle...*

Chapter 10

PRAYER FOR VICTORY WHEN A WOMAN SUFFERS MISCARRIAGES

Read: *Pro. 26:2; Ps. 24:1; Isa. 54:15-17; Gal. 6:17;*
Isa.59:1; Matt. 12:33, 37; Ex. 12:7.
Sing: ** How excellent is your name O Lord...*

Many pregnant women suffer miscarriages and a lot of them have not cared to make research into the root of the matter. It has been discovered that a lot of things which many times may be spiritual rather than physical can be the cause of this.

DIFFERENT CAUSES OF MISCARRIAGE IN PREGNANCY:

1. Excessive and strenuous work during pregnancy.
2. Taking hard drugs that has spoiled the womb either before or during pregnancy. This leads to abortion.
3. Bad dreams.
4. Pregnant woman having sex in the dream.
5. A pregnant woman seeing blood or red cloth in her dream.
6. A pregnant woman eating in her dream.
7. Old people appearing to a pregnant woman in her dream.
8. A pregnant woman delivering in her dream.

Sing: How excellent is your name O Lord...

THE RAIN OF PRAYERS

1. O Lord! expose the real foundation of miscarriage in my life, in Jesus' name *(Three times)*.
2. Everything in my life, that is causing me to miscarry, is set ablaze, in Jesus' name *(Seven times)*.

| 28 |

For Victory and Abundant Blessings in all life's situations

3. Whatever has been planted in me by the enemies making me to miscarry is burnt up right now, in Jesus' name.
4. I wash my womb now with the blood of Jesus, in Jesus' name *(do this for five minutes)*.
5. Every demon sucking my foetus, I command you to vanish now, in Jesus' name *(Seven times)*.
6. I shall conceive, it shall abide and I shall deliver my own baby, in Jesus' name.

Begin to give God the glory for your own baby.

Warning:
1. As soon as you have conceived, do not tell anyone; let God Himself reveal it.
2. Do not be involved in taking any herbs, spiritual bath, burning candle or incense or sacrificing your cloth. This is dangerous and it amounts to demonic covenant. Be careful, such children that came from these practices do not last and they also give lots of troubles to their parents. You are warned!
3. Do not wash your private parts with any charm or herb. Experience has made us to know that people who do such end up having children with familiar spirits, to their regret.
4. Examine your life; are you not in any cult? Have you ever been told that you were once initiated into a secret cult while you were a kid? Pray the prayers of deliverance, in this book, pray earnestly. Believe you are delivered. I trust my God that He has delivered you.

Begin to buy things for your coming child.

Sing: *You are the mighty God, the great I Am...*

| 29 |

Chapter 11

VICTORY OVER DIFFERENT COVENANTS AND CURSES

Read: II Sam 21:1, II King 2: 18-22 Col. 2:14-15; Gal. 3:13-14; II Cor. 6:14 – 18; Gal. 6:17; Zech. 2:5, Luke. 10:19.
Sing: * What can wash my sins away...

People enter into covenants ignorantly and in several ways. It may be through the name they bear, family cognomen, involvement in family cult, idolatry, making charm, sex, sin, spiritual bath, burning candles to pray, going to spiritual doctors, going to churches that are not of Jesus Christ, the Saviour of the world, making incision and using of one's cloth for sacrifice or prayer and so on. They are all covenants and treaties that give birth to curses in one's life.

Sing: * What can wash my sins away...

Different curses that afflict people:
1. Curse of law – Deut. 28:15-68.
2. Inherited and generational curse – Gen. 49:1.
3. Self-inflicted curse – Gen. 4:9, 13 – 15.
4. Curse from the wicked one, incantation, divination or evil spirit – Num. 23: 23.
5. Carelessness – Eccl. 5:4-9; Ps. 66:13.
6. Curse of the word of God – Ps. 17:13, II Sam. 12: 9-12.
7. Curse from entering into demonic covenant – II Sam. 21: 1-14.
8. Curse of labouring without reaping its reward.
9. Curse of stagnation (embargo).
10. Curse of scattering one's prosperity away.
11. Curse of early or premature death.

12. Curse that makes one's prosperity to waste away.
13. Curse that prevents one from measuring up to prosperity standard.
14. Curse that snatches one's rights.

Sing: ** I plead the blood, the blood of Jesus...*

Do these:
1. Place your hand on your head and plead the blood of Jesus for about two minutes.
2. Know and address the actual curse battling your life.
3. Look for the word of God on victory over what is bringing curses into your life.
4. Confess the sins that brought curses into your life and confess your faith in Jesus Christ as your Lord and Saviour.
5. Confess your separation from the known covenants and curses confronting you.

THE RAIN OF PRAYERS
1. My Lord, expose the secret of the actual curse afflicting my life today, in Jesus' name.
2. Lord, you are the curse remover, by your blood, block every way, by which family and generational curses are working evil in my life and job, and remove all curses from my life, in Jesus' name.
3. I bring myself out today; from all family curses and covenants that has been troubling my life for a long time, in Jesus' name.
4. Spirit behind the curse tormenting my life, I command you to get out of my life now, in Jesus' name *(Seven times).*
5. Lord, I command all generational curses afflicting my paternal and maternal families to stop from today, in Jesus' name
6. Every padlock of the enemy that has put my family and me in the bondage of curse is opened right now, in Jesus' name.
7. All covenants that my family might have entered into with herbalists or spiritualists that are bringing curses upon me, I destroy them with the blood of Jesus today, in Jesus' name.

8. Every curse placed on me and my family by the enemies up to ten generations forward and backwards, I destroy you with the blood of Jesus, in Jesus' name.
9. Every foundation of the curse that is causing failure in my life, receive the fire of God and be totally destroyed in Jesus' name.
10. By the power in the blood of Jesus, I command all generational, self-imposed curses working evil in my life, to be terminated now in Jesus' name.
11. Plead the blood of Jesus on your head for twenty-one times.
12. I destroy every association with covenants and curses troubling my life, in Jesus' name.
13. Call the blood of Jesus on your head for twenty-one times.

Sing: ** There is power mighty in the blood...*

■ For Victory and Abundant Blessings in all life's situations

Chapter 12

PRAYER OF VICTORY OVER FEAR, DISMAY, TERROR AND CONFUSION OF MIND

Read: Ps. 91:5, Deut. 31:8; Ps. 23:4; II Tim. 4:7; Isa. 41:10; Ps. 56:3; 11; Ps. 16:7-8.

Sing: * *Thou art worthy o Lord...*
* *Victory, Victory, Hallelujah...*
* *Into my heart...*

Beloved, if you are confused full of fear, dismayed or under terror, be sure it is not from God. It is the work of the devil. To overcome these demons operating against your life, pray the following prayers. Let me assure you that surely, if you pray, you will overcome these problems. As you wish to pray, first check your life, ask for forgiveness of all sins including disobedience to the word of God, and ask for cleansing by the blood of Jesus Christ. Know the problem you want to pray over and begin to pray. Place your hand on your chest and plead the blood of Jesus for three minutes.

THE RAIN OF PRAYERS

1. You spirit of (...)* in my life, God rebuke you, pack your load and get out of my life, in Jesus' name.
2. Every bondage of (...)* in my life, in my mind, be broken and get out, in Jesus' name. *Mention the name of the problem
3. I deliver myself from the battle of (...)* this day, in the name of Jesus Christ (Seven times).
4. You spirit of (...),* according to the word of God, I bind you and I command you to get out of my life now, in Jesus' name.
5. Every doorway through which (...)* is entering my life I close you up now, in Jesus' name.
6. Let the habitation of (...)* in my life and mind be demolished, in Jesus' name.

7. I wage war against you spirit of (...)* that operates through night, daytime, height, river, valley, insect, animal, birds, human beings, family, work, death, evil thought and so on, be set ablaze, in Jesus' name.
8. Plead the blood of Jesus on your mind to cleanse it, and tell the Holy Spirit to enter into your heart today.
9. Blood of Jesus, begin to wash my heart and cleanse it, in Jesus' name.
10. Lord, give me a new heart, in Jesus' name *(Twelve times)*.

Sing: ** Into.my heart twice come into my heart...*

Chapter 13

PRAYER OF DELIVERANCE FROM FINANCIAL AFFLICTION

Read: *III Jn. 2; Ps. 37:25; 34:10; 23:1; Duet. 28:2-8, 11-13;*
Luke 6:38; I Cor. 16:2; Matt. 10:8; Mal. 3:10-12; II Cor. 9:6-8;
Matt. 19:29, Josh. 1:8; Haggai 2:8; Eccl.2: 26; Pro. 13:22,
Duet. 8:7 – 14; 18; Matt. 6:31– 33; Phil. 4:19; Gen. 12:2-3.
Hag 2:8

Sing: *There shall be showers of blessing...*

Financial affliction is a common thing today in the world. Many have taken their own life just because of it. They have truly been working but still full of lack and in abject poverty. The demons of poverty and financial affliction are responsible for this. Sometimes, it is the curse of the enemy that opens door for these demons to operate but it is your own time to conquer if you will submit all to Christ Jesus. He will deliver you.

THE RAIN OF PRAYERS

1. Plead the blood of Jesus and call, Holy Ghost fire *(seven times)* and say: Lord, your promise is that it shall be well with me; therefore, I reject the spirit of lack and poverty in my life from today, in Jesus' name.
2. Spirit of Lack and Poverty, you are Satan's agents, I now command you to leave and get out of my life completely, in Jesus' name.
3. My God, release your power, to begin the work of blessing and creation of wealth in my life from today, in Jesus' name.
4. Lord, I really need money to fulfil responsibilities given to me by you, provide it for me in your miraculous ways and make me a source of blessing as from today on, in Jesus' name.
5. Father, send to me the wonder that terminates poverty in one's life,

For Victory and Abundant Blessings in all life's situations

in Jesus' name.
6. Lord, send me your financial help from mount Zion, in Jesus' name.
7. Divine provider, provide your own silver and gold, which will lead me into great prosperity as from today, in Jesus' name.
8. Today, my Lord, bless the work of my hand and rain down the blessing of money on me, in Jesus' name.
9. Father, as from today, I refuse to lack money and it shall be well with me, in Jesus 'name (Three times).
10. The Good Shepherd, make me to eat in the green pasture of your wealth today and give me the authority of comfort, in Jesus' name.
11. Gracious one, multiply your grace in my life today so much so that money shall be abundant on me, in Jesus' name.
12. My God, send gladdening financial news to me today, in Jesus' name (Seven times).
13. Lord, you provided money from the mouth of a fish in the time of Peter; provide money for me through blessed people, in Jesus' name *(Three times).*
14. God, cause a situation that will forever terminate poverty in my life today, in Jesus' name *(Three times).*
15. Money, you are God's messenger, therefore begin to find me out from today, in Jesus' name *(Three times).*
16. My Father, give me the wisdom to acquire and to spend money, in Jesus' name (Seven times).
17. My God, do not let me be put to shame concerning having money, take me to a higher ground, in Jesus' name.
18. Father, I completely reject the devourer and a life of poverty, in Jesus' name.

Sing: * *The Great Provider...*

■ For Victory and Abundant Blessings in all life's situations

Chapter 14

INABILITY TO GET WEALTH

Read: *Matt.12:28; Luke.9:1-2; Acts10:38; Gen.1:3: John. 1:1; Mk.11:23; Ps.17:4; Jn.14:23; Isa. 65:22.*
Sing: ** Abraham blessings are mine...*

It will be good if you can examine yourself critically. Do you partake in the work of the Gospel? Do you show mercy? Do you pay your tithes? If you have not been doing these, start today. You must also know that, it is God that gives wealth not how hard-working you are. So, as you work, pray and trust Him for your wealth. If you work and it is as if you are not, then you have to pray.

Sing: ** Abraham blessings are mine...*

PRAY THESE PRAYERS THREE TIMES:
1. Today, I confront all you powers that make me to sow without reaping, I face you with the battle of the Living God be destroyed to the root, in Jesus' name.
2. All family battles and other powers making my work to retrogress, father, let the fire of Holy Ghost consume them completely today, in Jesus' name.
3. Let the thunder of God strike those who gather against my success and life, and consume them, in Jesus' name.
4. I deliver myself completely today from you spirits that make one to work and toil only to make one suffer loss, in Jesus' name.
5. I refuse to work for my enemy to eat as from today, in Jesus' name *(Seven times).*
6. Lord, destroy the work of the enemy and the spirit of loss and shortage completely from my life, in Jesus' name.

| 37 |

7. Today, Lord, show me the way to breakthrough in my life, in Jesus' name.
8. Give me the heavenly wisdom to control wealth O Lord! in Jesus' name (Seven times).
9. All enemies against my exaltation, the Lord rebukes you all, in Jesus' name.
10. My Lord and Creator, make my work more untouchable for my enemies as from today, in Jesus' name.
11. Lord, honour me by your grace. This is my befitting time, in Jesus' name.
12. Father, give me the comfort of the body and the soul, and a diligent spirit that I may gather wealth to your glory, in Jesus' name.
13. Father, take the three key posts of; the chairman, director and accountant of my business and continue to run it from today, in Jesus' name.
14. Lord, everything I lay my hands on, let it prosper according to your word, in Jesus' name.
15. From now, my God, count me among your blessed ones, in Jesus' name.
16. Father, do not let Satan overcome in the affairs of my life, in Jesus' name.

Worship God with your resources and life. Have a record of what comes in and how it goes out. Make necessary correction. Be careful of favours that have no reward, that is, favour that is not prompted by God. Pray for God's direction. *Read Isaiah 1:19.*

Sing: * *The Great Provider...*

■ For Victory and Abundant Blessings in all life s situations

Chapter 15

PRAYER AGAINST ANGER AND EVIL THOUGHTS

Read: Jas.1:19-20; Eph.2:6; Pro.12:1; Matt.6:1,Pro.16:32; Eccl.7:9; Rom.12:19-24;Eph.4:31-32; Matt. 5:22-24, Pro.14:16-17; Col.3:8; Ps.37:8; Ps.18:48; Job5:2; Eph.4:27, 31.
Sing: **Lord I lift your name on high...**

Angry and evil thought are two things that have wrecked a lot of bright destinies in the past. They operate as demons under the spirit of destruction. They are destroyers. They make one to commit grievous mistake that may not be reversible. Have you been noticing them in your life? Then, it is time to destroy them before they destroy you. They act like dynamite, they are time-bombs, you cannot keep them for long, except you quickly do away with them, they will explode and destroy you. They appear in destruction of property, marital problem that leads to divorce, sexual immorality, fighting, hatred and so on. They also hinder blessings from coming to one.

PRAY THESE PRAYERS THREE TIMES:
1. Thank God for the death of Jesus Christ on the cross and worship God for at least five minutes
2. Ask for forgiveness of your sins.
3. Ask the Holy Spirit to take control of your life and breathe on you now.
4. Every root of anger in my life is uprooted now in the name of Jesus (Seven times).
5. You spirit of anger, the Lord rebukes you from my life. I bind you and command you to vanish from my life, in Jesus' name.
6. Father, I receive the grace to overcome this flesh of anger, in Jesus' name.

7. Every root of the love of evil things in my life is totally consumed, in Jesus' name.
8. Every bondage of anger is broken now in Jesus' name.
9. Blood of Jesus, begin to wash my heart; wash it clean, in Jesus' name.
10. Lord, give me a new heart and renew a right spirit within me, in Jesus' name *(Twelve times)*.
11. All the blessings that have eluded me as a result of anger are restored from now, in Jesus' name.
12. Holy Spirit, uphold me at all times that I may not make mistake, give me the spirit of watchfulness every time, in Jesus' name.
13. Lord, put your guard around my heart to keep it from evil thought.
14. I close every entrance by which evil thoughts creep into my mind, in Jesus' name.
15. Lord, let the presence of God fills my mind and keep my heart clean, in Jesus' name.

Sing: Into my life Spirit of the Living God...

Chapter 16

PRAYER AGAINST FAILURE AND DISAPPOINTMENT

Read: Zech. 4:9; Phil.1: 6; 2:13; Jude 24-25; Gen. 24:12-14; 26:27; Exo.11: 2-3; Ps.16: 5; 138:8; Phil.4: 19.
Sing: Let God arise...

The spirits of failure and disappointment are troubling a lot of people but they erroneously think it is the will of God, whereas they are wrong. Did you begin a project but you cannot complete it? Or you have an occasion before you and right from when a date has been fixed for this occasion, evil things have been happening? Or you have been doing a particular thing over and over without success, watch yourself very well; it is the work of the enemy. Certainly, you need prayers of deliverance.

Sing: Let God arise...

PRAY THESE PRAYERS THREE TIMES:
1. Plead the blood of Jesus on yourself for three minutes and say:
2. My Lord, expose to me the root of failure and disappointment in my life, in Jesus' name.
3. Everything hindering the progress of my life, I destroy you all with the power in the blood of Jesus, in Jesus' name.
4. All spirits of failure and disappointment, I uproot you from my life, in Jesus' name.
5. You pillar of failure in my life; I destroy you today, in Jesus' name *(Seven times)*.
6. I call the fire of the Holy Ghost to consume all entanglements of failure and disappointment from my life from now on, in Jesus' name.
7. I confront all spirits blocking my blessing and working together with

the spirits of failure and disappointment against my life to be wiped out, in Jesus' name. You spirit of disappointment, you are an illegal power in my life, therefore, be destroyed, in Jesus' name.

8. Let the blood of Jesus begin to cancel the mark of failure in my life right now, in Jesus' name.
9. I cancel my own name with the blood of Jesus from the register book of failure, in Jesus' name.
10. You heavenly insurance committee, begin to put all the losses of my life to total shame right now, in Jesus' name.
11. As rivulet *(a small stream)* locates the river, let all the blessings of my life that were gone begin to find me out from all areas, in Jesus' name.
12. Every cloth of non-accomplishment, and disappointment that the enemy has put on me, be destroyed by Holy Ghost fire, in Jesus' name.
13. Fire of the Holy Spirit, consume everything causing go slow in my life, in my family and my work, in Jesus' name.
14. As from today, all obstructions to my success are removed, in Jesus' name.
15. Form today, all my good fortunes that have been lost are restored to me, in Jesus' name.
16. From today, all curses of failure and disappointment upon my life are destroyed by the power in the blood of Jesus, in Jesus' name.
17. I confess that goodness, success and exaltation are mine from today on, in Jesus' name.

Sing: * ***Blessed be the name of the Lord...***
  * ***I have a Father that will never never fail me...***

For Victory and Abundant Blessings in all life's situations

Chapter 17

DEBT, DEVOURER, SALES BLOCKER AND ASSOCIATE PROBLEMS

Read: Ex. 3:20; II Kings 4:1-7; Phil. 4:19; Isa.45: 13; I Sam. 30:8.
Sing: * Oh glory, glory to the Lord...
      * What shall I render...

Debt, devourer and sales blocking spirits are all evil spirits that Satan uses to put people in restlessness of mind. Therefore, arrest the demons because the word of God, says *"...resist the devil and he will flee"* (James 4:7). If you want to receive deliverance from debt, devourer and sales blocker, first you have to examine yourself very well in the line of the following truths:

- Have you received Jesus Christ into your life as your Lord and Saviour? – *John. 3:16.*
- Do you pay your tithes regularly? – *Mal. 3:8-12*
- Do you give to the needy cheerfully? There are many blessings in it – *Deut. 28:46-48.*
- Plant in the work of the Gospel and try to pray over your work – *Luke. 6:38.*
- Do not steal and do not be lazy, it is very bad – *Pro. 6:6-10.*

PRAY THESE PRAYERS THREE TIMES:

1. God, my helper in times of trouble, stretch forth your mighty hand over my life today and more importantly on this debt confronting me and give me victory, in Jesus' name.
2. I plead the blood of Jesus to remove every mark of (...)* in my life, in Jesus' name.
3. Every demon of (...)*in my life, I command the ground to swallow you up and never to lift up your ugly head again, in Jesus' name.

For Victory and Abundant Blessings in all life's situations

4. Let the love for debt be totally removed from my heart, in Jesus' name.
5. O Lord! I receive the power to overcome this debt, in the name of Jesus.
6. The bondage of indebtedness is broken in my life today, in Jesus' name.
7. The curse of indebtedness I inherited and the one I caused by myself, I reject you all and I wage war against you. By the blood of Jesus, be totally removed now, in Jesus' name.
8. You heavenly insurance committee (Father, Son and Holy Spirit) begin to remove the shame, that loss, debt, devourer and sales blocker have caused in my life, in Jesus' name.
9. You heavenly insurance committee, convert my crying to laughter now, in Jesus' name.
10. Lord, whether Satan likes it or not, take me to my shore of success, a safe harbour, in Jesus' name.
11. I release and receive my freedom from the society of debtors today, in Jesus' name.

Sing: *Come what may, Jesus shall reign...*

Chapter 18

PRAYER OF VICTORY OVER OBSTACLES AND OBSTRUCTIONS ON YOUR WAY

Read: Isa. 8:9-10; 49:24-26; 54:15-17; Joshua 6; Ex. 14; Esther 7; Ps. 24.
Sing: *Arise o Lord! let my enemies be scattered...*

The spirit of obstruction is a hindrance to success and progress they are instruments the Devil uses to bring failure, stagnancy, backwardness or disappointment into people's lives. For you to conquer, speed up these prayers with three days fasting, praying on three hourly basis. Also, examine yourself, is there no sin obstructing the goodness of God in your life?

PRAY THESE PRAYERS THREE TIMES:
1. Father, all roots and causes of obstruction, obstacles and blockages in my life, expose them, in Jesus' name.
2. Father, all obstacles known and unknown obstructing the blessings of my life, let the Holy Ghost fire scatter and consume them, in Jesus' name.
3. All enemies who are like walls of Jericho in my life, family and work, Father, let them be swallowed up by the ground and never to rise again, and let ways be opened for me, in Jesus' name.
4. All roots of the devil, obstacles and obstructions in my life, be uprooted now and be set ablaze, in Jesus' name.
5. All deceitful friends obstructing the blessings of my life, Lord, sweep them away from my life and separate me completely from them, in Jesus' name.
6. All enemies threatening my entering into the Promised Land, Lord, put them into the problem of *"it is not easy"*, in, Jesus' name.
7. All doors of my blessing and divine exaltation that the enemy has closed, be opened now, in Jesus' name.

For Victory and Abundant Blessings in all life's situations

8. Lord, make me fire in the hands of my enemies from today. Make me one that cannot be caught or hurt by them, in Jesus' name.
9. Let all my enemies fall into the pit they have dug for me, in Jesus' name.
10. Father, before the daybreaks, destroy my enemies completely, in Jesus' name.
11. You enemies causing obstructions and obstacles in my life, begin to die off, in Jesus' name.
12. My God, you walked with the Israelites and their enemies perished; Walk with me too and let all my enemies perish.
13. All you enemies that follow me about and pursue relentlessly, hear the word of God and dry up quickly, in Jesus' name.
14. Certainly, I (*) shall get to where my prosperity is, in Jesus' name.
15. God let there be ways of prosperity open for me from now on, in Jesus' name.
16. According to the word of God, let your presence encompasses me, in Jesus' name.

The battle is over, rejoice (Phil. 4:4) and start singing this song unto the Lord.

Sing: * **God has made a way where there seems to be no way...**
 * **We thank you Lord (twice), we thank you Jehovah Almighty...**

For Victory and Abundant Blessings in all life's situations

Chapter 19

VICTORY OVER THE SPIRIT OF DEATH

Read: *Ps. 118:17; 23:4; 27: 1-3; 91; Duet. 33:25-27;*
John.10:10; 6:35-40; Rom. 8:18-39; II Tim. 4:18; Phil. 4:13;
Col.2: 14; Job 19:25; Gal.6: 17.

Sing: ** Victory, Victory Hallelujah...*

Anytime the thought of death comes to your mind or someone sees a vision of death concerning you or you see coffin or dead people, pray these prayers with fasting over the matter. Use the prayer of deliverance after having read and meditated on the scriptural passages above.

Sing: *Oh glory, glory, glory to the Lord...*

PRAY THESE PRAYERS:

1. Begin to glorify God for your life in Jesus Christ. Call the name of Jesus seven times and the blood of Jesus twenty-one times.
2. With the power in the blood of Jesus, I destroy now every covenant of death concerning my family, and me *(Three times).*
3. O Lord! you that removed the name of king Hezekiah from the book of death, remove my name and that of my family from the register of death today, in Jesus' name *(Seven times).*
4. You spirit of death, turn back from me now, in Jesus' name.
5. Death, I command you to go away from my family and me, in Jesus' name.
6. I will not die any death, but I will live for the glory of God, in Jesus' name *(Seven times).*
7. It is compulsory for me to be useful for God, therefore, you spirit of death and Satan, I rebuke you; get out of my life now, in Jesus name *(Seven times).*

| 47 |

8. Call the blood of Jesus for about three minutes. Use the blood to mark yourself and say: no death should trouble me anymore, in Jesus' name.
9. Holy Spirit, enter into my heart now, in Jesus' name *(do this for about three minutes.)*
10. You death, listen to the word of God, the person that sent you to me, to my wife, to my child, go back now and deliver that very message to the person, in Jesus' name.
11. The trap of death that the enemy has set for me, let the enemy himself or herself fall into it, in Jesus' name.
12. Begin to praise God with your whole heart.
13. The Bible says my covenant with death has been disannulled, therefore, you spirit of death be destroyed from my life in Jesus' name.
14. I shall not die but live, in Jesus name.
15. I have given my life to Jesus, and He has come to give me life, for death is of the devil for he has come to kill and I am not a son to the devil, therefore, I reject death in Jesus' name.

Sing: * *Alive, alive, my Saviour is alive...*

■ For Victory and Abundant Blessings in all life's situations

Chapter 20

FAVOUR OF GOD IN EVERY WAY

Read: Ps. 27:1; Ps. 23:6; Ps. 62:5
Sing: Adonai, I worship you...

Many people who should be favoured are faced with hatred, disappointment and hostility today. A lot have seen with their eyes (face to face) their blessing but were denied by the enemy. At the door of success, many have been turned back because the enemy breezed in. Disfavour can be as a result of curse, sin or attack of the enemy, but you can ask God today to break the yoke of hostility and disappointment through the blood of Jesus.

PRAY THESE PRAYERS:
1. Praise God for who He is, confess your sins and iniquities. Thank Him for all He has done and all He will do in your life,
2. Lord, put your power and garment of favour on me today, in Jesus' name.
3. Whatever the enemy has planted between my goodness and me, Lord, uproot it and set it ablaze completely, in Jesus' name.
4. I reject every spirit of hostility and disappointment from those who should favour me, in Jesus' name.
5. Lord, look upon me with favour from today, in Jesus' name.
6. Father, find me out with your special favour, in Jesus' name.
7. O God, you caused the Israelites to be favoured by the Egyptians, let me too receive favour from everyone I meet today, in Jesus' name.
8. From every area, North, South, East and West, Father let me receive favour, in Jesus' name.
9. Holy Spirit, put your mark of favour on me today, in Jesus' name.

10. That person you have appointed to bless my life, Lord, cause us to meet each other today, in Jesus' name.
11. At every place where I have been rejected and forsaken, Lord, by the reason of your favour let me become a star, in Jesus' name.
12. It is joy and gladness that always, attend the birth of a new baby, my Lord, from today, by the reason of your favour, make me to become a man of honour and praise everywhere I go, in Jesus' name.
13. As rivulet (small stream) finds its way to the river, by your favour, let my goodness, joy and miracles find me out today, in Jesus' name.
14. Within and without and everywhere, I shall always meet favour, in Jesus' name.

Begin to praise the King of kings because your prayers are answered according to your faith. Favour is from God, not man. It is only the divine favour that comes from the Father that lasts. Therefore, look unto God and have faith in Him. He will surely bestow this favour on you, in Jesus' name.

Sing: ** He is a miracle working God...*

Chapter 21

VICTORY OVER BARRENNESS

Read: *Jer. 32:27; Deut. 7:13-15, Exo. 12:7; 23:25-26; Eccl. 11:5; Ps. 113:9; Gal.3: 13; 6:17; Rom. 8:11; Heb. 9:19 – 21.*
Sing: ** I have a God who never fails...*

Barrenness is a curse of law, but however bad it may be, if you can accept Jesus Christ as your Lord and Saviour, there will be a way out. He has redeemed you from the curse of barrenness; therefore, do not accept bareness in your life *(James 4:7)*. You are fruitful and not barren, believe and confess this. Confess the sins of any abortion or the use of hard drugs in the past *(Study Ps. 51 and 32)*. Of a truth, there are different causes of barrenness. Some of them are the sins of abortion, vengeance, family curse, spiritual husband, deceitful spirit, pride, disease, snatching another woman's husband, unforgiveness, fear or doubt, covenant making, refusing to pay vow, hatred to others and so on. Have you undergone deliverance over this matter? Look for a true Bible believing Church of God and tell them your situation, confess all you have done contrary to the law of God. Ask for prayers of deliverance. After these prayers believe in your heart that the battle is over and that God has answered you.

Sing: I have a God who never fails...

PRAY THESE PRAYERS:
Pray this way everyday until you are pregnant. Backup the prayer with seven days fasting and three hourly prayers. Do it in faith. During and after conception continue in prayer. Plead the blood of Jesus on yourself for some time. *Place your hand on your belly as you pray these prayers and call the blood of Jesus twenty-one times.*
1.   Spirit of barrenness, I wage war against you today, in my life, in Jesus' name.

| 51 |

2. I bind and command you spirit of barrenness to get out of my life today, in Jesus' name *(Seven times)*.
3. I deliver myself from the bondage and fear of pregnancy, in Jesus' name.
4. I command that my organs and that of my spouse should receive perfect deliverance now, in Jesus' name. I command all aspects of our reproductive systems that have been damaged by reason of satanic activities, to receive healing, and be put in their normal position, in Jesus' name. Lord Jesus, renew every organ in our bodies. Open the door for children to come to earth through us. Remove all our reproaches and cancel all embarrassments and shame, in Jesus' name.
5. I stand against every evil report of medical doctors over my case, in Jesus' name.
6. From this hour, I command every part of my body that is dead, to be alive by the power of the Holy Ghost, in Jesus' name *(Seven times)*.
7. My womb, be prepared to hold baby for the next nine months according to the plan and design of God, in Jesus' name.
8. Start saying, **"I have become a fruitful woman to the glory of the Living God, in Jesus' name."**

Sing: I have a very big God o...

Remember Sarah, as old as she was, Elizabeth and Manoah's wife, they all became mothers, Hallelujah! Yours too will not be difficult; believe in God *(Mk. 9:23)* have faith, do not doubt. **Read 1 Sam 1*.** Begin to confess that you are a mother. Also, begin to buy baby wares. I plead with you in the name of the Lord; do not broadcast yourself about, the moment you conceive. Please be reserved and keep sealed lips. Remember the mother of Jesus, when she was told she was going to give birth to the Saviour of the world *(the Bible says she did not tell anyone)*. Remain silent, Joseph the dreamer disclosed his dream, and the enemy tried in all ways to destroy his vision. The moment you conceive, just be praying and praising God. You may write to us in order that we may lift you up in prayer. It shall be well with you, in Jesus' name. Amen.

Chapter 22

OVERCOMING LONG-STANDING PROBLEMS

Read: Zech. 4:7; Ps. 2:9; Deut. 3:27; Ps. 109; 17:29; Isa. 49:25-26; Ps. 129:5-6; Joshua 6; 10:8-11.

Sing: *Arise O Lord, let my enemy be scattered...*

Long-standing problem is as a result of unrelenting spirit of the enemy but you can break the yoke today in prayer. Praise God and exalt Him. Confess your sins and plead the blood of Jesus for your cleansing. Have you prayed for seven days over this problem before? Try this with three hourly prayers for seven days. After these seven days, you will see the victory of the Lord.

Sing: *Arise O Lord, let your enemy be scattered...*

PRAY THESE PRAYERS:

1. Call the name and the blood of Jesus seven times each, and say: Lord my God, reveal the hidden secret behind my problems to me, in Jesus' name *(Seven times)*.
2. You long-standing problem in my life, hear the word of the Lord, I rebuke you from my life and I part from you today, in Jesus' name *(Three time)*.
3. Every committee of enemies behind the problems of my life, the Lord scatters you all today, in Jesus' name.
4. I command the fire of the Lord to begin to burn and consume all the enemies behind the problems of my life now, in Jesus' name.
5. Plead the blood of Jesus over yourself for two minutes.
6. You host of heaven, fiery angels of God who kill without regard to number, begin to terminate the works of my enemies, in Jesus' name.

7. Say: *"Jesus is Lord"* for about five minutes.
8. O earth!, earth!!, hear the word of God, out of you, man was created, you are God's creature of the third day, anyone born of woman eating and sleeping on you that is behind my problem, open up and swallow such one, in Jesus' name.
9. Every battle that is saying *"No"* to where God says *"Yes"* in my life is torn into pieces, in Jesus' name.
10. All the battles called *"No"*, co-operating against the goodness of my life, be set ablaze now, in Jesus' name.
11. All who obstruct my progress and have made themselves the *"I am"* in my life, earth, open up and swallow them, in Jesus' name.
12. Every battle I have made effort to appease but have refused to go, God destroy it, in Jesus' name.
13. The wizard, witch or ogbanje that is troubling me, fire of God consume him or her completely, in Jesus' name
14. All battles that gather around and cooperate against the affairs of my life, storm of heaven, sweep them away, in Jesus' name.
15 Lord, strike like thunder, operate like whirlwind, and uproot all trees of the enemies bearing evil fruits in my life, in Jesus' name.

Ask for the infilling of the Holy Spirit. Ask the Holy Spirit to manifest His power in your life and begin to thank God for this victory.

Sing: * *Messiah is the king of king...*

Chapter 23

ENEMY WHO PURSUES RELENTLESSLY

Read: Exo.14:23-31; Isa 47:9; Joshua 10:8-11
Sing: Let the power of the Lord comes down...

There are some enemies that pursue relentlessly; they are like Balaam the son of Beor who wanted to curse the people of God by all means (Numb.22). They make a man to continue in battle through-out lifetime. When one is overcoming a battle, they introduce another. You can conquer them today if you will pray.

PRAY THESE PRAYERS:
1. Praise God with the song that comes to your mind.
2. Confess your sins and ask God for forgiveness.
3. Call God to look down from heaven and fall upon all enemies who pursue relentlessly, in order to snatch your goodness.
4. Lord, consider the affairs of my life this very day and send help to me, in Jesus' name.
5. Every problem in my life over which the enemy is taking delight and boasting, Father, destroy them and their power, in Jesus' name.
6. Father, prove yourself that the enemy may know that you are my God. Do sudden wonders and miracles for me, in Jesus' name.
7. All enemies who refuse to stop pursuing my job and family, let the Red Sea swallow them up, in Jesus' name.
8. All the instruments helping my enemies, let the Red Sea swallow them up, in Jesus' name.
9. O Lord! let the hands of all the relentless enemies feeding me with food of sorrow and water of affliction, dry off, in Jesus' name
10. Father, frighten and terrorise all the enemies troubling me. Do not let them have peace in their hearts from now on, in Jesus' name.

11. Lord, fill the mouths of my enemies with shouts of horror and replace my weeping with joy and laughter, in Jesus' name.
12. All enemies who are working together to destroy my life, Lord; sweep them away, in Jesus' name.
13 Lord, send the terrible host of angels into the midst of my relentless enemies today, in Jesus' name.
1   All the battles of the enemies who have pitched their tents around me, today, Lord, send them to the abyss, in Jesus' name.
15. All enemies that do not want me to get to my point of miracle; I command the earth to swallow them, in Jesus' name.
16. All the battles of life that want to make my life a failure are consumed, in Jesus' name.
17. I command terrible disasters that cannot be forgotten, to begin to happen to enemies that refuse to turn back from pursuing me, in Jesus' name.
18. As offices always outlive office workers, I receive the power to see the end of my enemies, in Jesus' name.

Confess that Jesus Christ is your Lord for twenty-one times. Thank God for He has heard you. Begin to praise Him with songs of praise and thanksgiving.

Sing: Because He lives, I can face...

Chapter **24**

PRAYERS TO CONFRONT EVERY POWER OF THE ENEMY OVER YOUR WORK

Read: *Isa. 8:9-10; Jer. 23:19; Ps. 68:1*
Sing: *Take glory Father...*

When your work is facing confrontation from the power of the enemy, you are working but the result is failure, then you have to pray. You must also first check and see that the work you are doing is one approved by God and in line with His heart, that is, not dubious and evil, the right work that can receive the blessing of God.

PRAY THESE PRAYERS:
1. Father, I destroy the evil hands of the enemies from my work today, and I become victorious over them, in Jesus' name.
2. All powers of darkness that have gathered over my work through curses and negative utterances, I confront you all now in the name of Jesus. I command fire from heaven to consume you all, in Jesus' name.
   Lord, draw my work out of affliction, confusion and trouble that the enemy has thrown it into, today. Remove all the hands of the enemies, from my work, in Jesus' name.
   Lord, by your mighty hand, I destroy the works of the devil totally from my life, in Jesus' name.
5. My Lord, enlarge my work, in Jesus' name.
6. Lord, increase my joy to the fullest over my work and do not allow the enemy to make me weep over it, in Jesus' name.
7. O Lord, I destroy confusion from my work and I receive jobs that will change my life for good, today, in Jesus' name.
8. Exalt me O Lord! in my work, and give me power to overcome all the enemies of progress that are against me, in Jesus' name.

| 57 |

9. I reject termination of job appointment and I stand against all enemies of progress in this work, in Jesus' name.
10. I command all devourers in my work to vanish as from today, in Jesus' name.
11. O God! lift me from the present position in this work to a higher level, in Jesus' name.
12. Lord, use your greatness over my life, and let me be successful, in Jesus' name.
13. I receive from you Lord, the power to breakthrough in this work, in Jesus' name.
14. O God! remove the hand of poverty from my life. Put me in a higher place, in Jesus' name.
15. Holy Spirit, exalt me in my work, with it, let me be blessed, in Jesus' name.
16. The big job that terminates poverty, affliction and suffering, Lord, provide it for me this week, this month and this year, in Jesus' name.
17. Lord, remove every spiritual and physical embargo placed on the progress of my work from today on, in Jesus' name.
18. I receive from the Lord, miracles that cannot be hidden in this work, in Jesus' name.
19. Lord, I receive my own good portion from this work, in Jesus' name.
20. O Lord! arise over my work and glorify yourself in it, in Jesus' name.

Sing: ** Victory, Victory...*

Chapter 25

PRAYER OVER DIFFERENT BATTLES OF THE ENEMY IN ONE'S LIFE

Read: *Jas. 4:7; Zech.4: 5; Ps. 68:1; Jn.8: 32; Ps.71;*
Isa.8:9-10; 54:15-17; Jer23: 19.
Sing: *The Lord reigneth...*

Different stage different battle, so it is for some people. But some face more than they expected at a single stage of their life. For them, it is always overwhelming and it is only the power of God through prayer that can deliver such ones. Just hand over everything to Jesus today. Tell Him you are surrendering all, He will help you.

PRAY THESE PRAYERS:
Mention the battle(s) confronting you and hand them over to Jesus Christ.

1. Call the blood of Jesus for about five minutes; use it to wash yourself from the head to toe.
2. Spend some time to ask for the power of Holy Spirit to refresh you again.
3. Father, expose the secret of where the battle of my life comes from, in Jesus' name *(Two times)*.
4. Arise O God and scatter all the enemies of my life, in Jesus' name *(Seven times)*.
5. I command all signs and marks of the battle of the enemy in my life to be washed away by the blood of Jesus, in Jesus' name *(Three times)*.
6. Lord, turn me to fire in the hands of my enemies and make me invisible before them, in Jesus' name. I envelope myself with the fire of Holy Ghost now in Jesus' name *(Three times)*.
7. Father, make me victorious, so that I may glorify you before my enemies, in Jesus' name.

8. Father, uproot and sweep away all the battles confronting my life, in Jesus' name – *Matt. 13:26 (Seven times).*
9. Lord, fight for me against all enemies rebelling against me secretly and openly, in Jesus' name *(Acts 23:12-13).*
10. All the evil works of the enemies directed at me, begin to go back to the senders, in Jesus' name *(Ps. 7:16; Esther 7:7-10).*
11. Lord, kindle your fire on every power of darkness working evil against me and set them ablaze, in Jesus' name *(Zech 2:5).*
12. I command the fire of God to fall upon and nullify all powers of curses, charms, idols and evil spirits in the heavenlies, in the water and beneath the earth on the issue of my life, in Jesus' name.
13. Just as the counsel of Ahitophel against David was frustrated by God, let all the battles of the enemies against my life be frustrated, in Jesus' name.
14. Lord, take away every strange mark of the enemy on me, today, in Jesus' name.
15. Every battle that makes the head to become the tail, Father take them away, in Jesus' name.
16. I overcome all the battles of the enemy in my life, in Jesus' name *(Seven times).*

ENSURE THAT *you too do not wage war against anyone except the devil and his work. Also do not wage war against yourself by going into sin.*

Sing: ** Victory, victory, hallelujah...*

■ For Victory and Abundant Blessings in all life s situations

Chapter 26

PRAYER FOR PREGNANT WOMEN

Read: Isa. 59:1, Ps.125: 1-2; 105:14-15; 127:3; 54:15-17;
Zech. 9:11; Rev. 12:11; Ex. 12:7.

Sing: * *I plead the blood, the blood of Jesus...*

Different battles do face pregnant women. Many a time the enemy desires to destroy the pregnancy, change the fruit in their womb or make it a disable. Traditionally, in Africa and some other continents of the world, a child could be attacked and changed to other things by the wicked people through diabolic means. Can you imagine? For these reasons, pregnant women need prayers at all times.

Sing: Let your living water flow...

PRAY THESE PRAYERS:
1. Place your hand on the pregnancy and call the blood of Jesus on yourself fourteen times and say:
2. Fire of the Holy Spirit of the Most High; cover me now, in Jesus' name *(Seven times)*.
3. That which is in this womb of mine is given to me by God and shall not be destroyed, in Jesus' name *(Three times)*.
4. All you evil spirits that terminate pregnancy, the fire of God consume you all now, in Jesus' name *(Three times)*.
5. Jesus is the Lord of this pregnancy, He is the owner of the baby in my womb *(Seven times) (Declare it powerfully)*.
6. All enemies trying to destroy this pregnancy are scattered, in Jesus' name *(Seven times)*.
7. I decree that no evil shall befall this baby in my womb, in Jesus' name *(Three times)*.

8. I shall deliver this baby normally at the appropriate time, in Jesus' name *(Seven times)*.
9. On the day of my delivery, I shall not tarry in labour, in Jesus' name.
10. I shall deliver safely, whoever does not want me to deliver safely, Lord, wage war against him or her in Jesus' name.
11. The Bible says, the Lord's hand is not shortened that it cannot save, therefore, all hands of the evil ones upon my pregnancy, begin to loose now, in the name of Jesus Christ.
12. Jesus Christ said, make a tree good and its fruit will be good. The blood of Jesus has made me a good tree by faith in Jesus. Therefore, the fruit in me must be good. Children are the heritage of the Lord, the fruit of the womb is its reward. The fruit of my womb is my reward. Likewise, the fruit of my womb shall not see corruption, in the name of Jesus.

Be praising God at all times and be careful of evil thoughts, do not allow them in your mind, you are victorious, in Jesus name. When the miracle happens, please, remember to write us to rejoice with you.

Sing: ** Thank you Jesus...*

Chapter 27

WHEN YOUR SPOUSE IS UNFAITHFUL AND TROUBLESOME

Read: Prov. 21:1-2; Job 22:28; Jer.10: 23.
Sing: * Covenant keeping God...*

The battle confronting some people is not that of money or health, but that of the unfaithfulness of their spouses. But, let it be known to you that, God created that unfaithful person. Even if the enemies have recreated him, Jesus has the power to change him or her for better. Believe, and your miracle will surely happen. You will recover him or her in Jesus' name *(Amen)*.

Sing: * Covenant keeping God...*

PRAY THESE PRAYERS:

1. Begin to exalt God over this problem and believe He will perform wonders for you.
2. Confess the sins you have committed through your bad character your word and careless attitude toward your spouse.
3. O Lord, you are the creator of heaven and earth, this is not the original person I married in the beginning, therefore, Lord, stretch forth your miraculous hand to change(...)* life, in Jesus' name *(Seven times)*.
4. The heart of the king is in your hand O my God, change the heart of (...)*for good, in Jesus' name. *(Three times)*.
5. Every spirit of hatred in the heart of (...),* I bind you and I command you to get out of him/her, in Jesus' name *(Three times)*.
6. The wall of separation between me and (...),* like the walls of Jericho, begin to fall and sink, in Jesus' name. *(Seven times)*.
7. Holy Spirit, change the life of (...)* for good, in Jesus name *(Seven times)*.

8. I command the first love between me and (...)*, to return and be restored permanently, in Jesus' name *(Seven times).*
9. I release genuine love into our family, in Jesus' name.
10. My God, make our home untouchable for the enemies, in Jesus' name.
11. Lord, make our home a good example to others, in Jesus' name.
12. I stand against the spirit of strange women and men in this home, in Jesus' name.
13. I frustrate every effort of the kingdom of darkness in breaking our home, in Jesus' name.

Begin to praise God with songs. Submit to the word of God. If you are the husband, love your wife according to the word of God and do not be bitter against her *(Col.3: 19, I Pet. 3:7).* You wife, submit to your husband, you husband love your wife for this is the will of God *(I Pet 3:1-6).*

NOTE: If you love someone you will be loyal to him or her no matter what it costs. You will always believe him or her, pray for him, or her without ceasing expect the best of him or her and always stand your ground in his or her defence (I Corinthians 13:7) Think on this!

Sing: ** O Lord! I am very very grateful, for all you have done for me...(Three times)*

Chapter **28**

PRAYER FOR ALL STUDENTS AND THOSE GOING FOR INTERVIEW OR EXAMINATION

Read: Jas. 3:17; Dan. 1:17, 20; Ps. 119:99; I Kings 3:12;
Ex. 31:2-3, 6, Jn. 6:63, Ps. 75:6 Rm. 8:11, Eph. 1:5-6,
I Jn. 5:4-5; Gen. 22:17, Esther 6:13; Rom. 5:17; Isa. 7:7.

Sing: * *What shall I do today...*
* *I have a God, who never fails...*

The Bible says, if any man lacks wisdom let him ask God. Wisdom, understanding and knowledge all belong to God. As students or somebody seeking higher ground or promotion, we need wisdom, understanding and knowledge from God. We also need the power to prosper and the spirit of success, ask and you will be given. Good things do not come from the East nor from the West but from God the giver of all good things. He said, I am the one that makes you to prosper. A life committed into the hand of God cannot fail. You are not a failure even though devil may be saying you are one but the word of God says No, you are not.

Sing: * *I have a Father, who can never never fail me...*
* *Since I believe in Jesus name...*

PRAY THESE PRAYERS:

1   Praise God for some time.
2   Place your hand on your head and call the blood of Jesus for about two minutes.
3   Now call upon the Lord your God, say: O Lord! give me your own wisdom and all I need for my studies, in Jesus' name *(Three times).*
4   Certainly, I need your understanding for my studies, Lord grant me, in Jesus' name.

5. Concerning this examination, I bind all the spirits of obstruction, failure and confusion, in Jesus' name.
6. I put on the whole armour of God and I destroy all the works of the devil over this examination, in Jesus' name.
7. With the blood of Jesus, I destroy everything called failure, in Jesus' name.
8. Every seed of failure over this examination is consumed by fire, in Jesus' name.
9. Spirit of failure, I reject you, in Jesus' name.
10. In this examination, I shall be met with the divine favour of God, in Jesus' name.
11. Holy Spirit (three times), in this examination and interview let me meet your mercies and the favour of the people, in Jesus' name.
12. Yes, in Jesus' name, I will make it *(Seven times)*.
13. Holy Spirit, revive my brain, spirit and mind today, in Jesus' name – Jn.6: 63, Rm.8: 11 *(Seven times)*.
14. Lord, let the spirit of success come upon me, in Jesus' name *(Seven times)*.
15. As the Psalmist had insight, Lord, give me insight more insight than my teachers, in Jesus' name *(Ps. 119:99)*.
16. O my Father! Daniel was ten times better than his mates, therefore, make me ten times better than my mates in this examination, in Jesus' name *(Ten times)*.
17. Holy Spirit (three times), let me see your favour in my entire examinations, in Jesus' name.
18. Among many people, let my success become possible, in Jesus' name *(Seven times)*.
19. As the Spirit of God filled Bezalel the son of Hur to perform excellently well, God fill me with your Holy Spirit, in Jesus' name *(Seven times)*.
20. I thank God for the exaltation I begin to have from now, in Jesus' name.

Sing: *Do something new in my life...*

HOW TO PASS AN EXAMINATION
1. Study very well and do more research.
2. Prepare for the examinations. Remember that prior planning prevent poor performance.
3. Pray well, eat well and sleep well.
4. Cover the syllabus.
5. Discuss with others.
6. Use past questions to prepare.
7. Be hardworking.
8. Do not worry during the examinations (Philippians 4:6)
9. Manage your time effectively during the examinations.
10. Pray to God for abundant life in Jesus Christ and you will not regret it at all.

Sing: ** Holy Spirit, do it now.*

Chapter 29

FOR ALL CONTRACTORS

Read: Phil. 4:19; Ps. 24:1; Ps. 89:34
Sing: * I have a Father, who never fails me...

God can connect you if you will talk to Him. It is the connection that God makes that brings great profit and lasts. He has the key to your door of success. The Holy Spirit knows where there is contract for you. You need to move closer to God and you will have a blessed time with Him.

PRAY THESE PRAYERS:
1. Praise God for a few minutes, confess your past sins and thank God for all good things in your life.
2. Begin to thank God for the entire blessing you have received in the past.
3. I put my faith in God concerning this contract, I declare, it shall be mine, in Jesus' name *(Three times)*.
4. All strongholds and walls of Jericho standing against this contract, I command you to collapse and sink into the ground, in Jesus' name.
5. The Bible says whoever does not work should not eat, Lord, give me this Job that I may get money to serve you, take care of my family and get food to eat according to your command, in Jesus' name.
6. This contract, I claim you by faith in Jesus' name *(Seven times)*.
7. Lord, arise for my help over this job, in Jesus' name.
8. As rivulet (small stream) finds river, let contracts begin to find me out from the North, South, East and West, in Jesus' name *(Three times)*.
9. Father, I command sudden goodness, unexpected miracle, ready-

made goodness, job that terminates poverty, to come to me, in Jesus' name. *(Seven times)*.
10. The door that leads to big contract be opened to me now, in Jesus' name.
11. You wind from God that always blows goodness to the children of God, blow big contracts to me now, in Jesus' name.
12. O Lord, make it impossible for anyone to cause my failure concerning this job, in Jesus' name.
13. *(Cry aloud and say):* Lord! *(Three times)* connect me afresh to a business that will remove poverty from my life forever.

NOTE:
1. Do not doubt about winning the contract
2. Believe that in Jesus, all things are possible *(Mk. 9:23)*.
3. Back these prayers with three days fasting.
4. Pray these prayers day and night.
5. Enter into covenant with God over what you will do, should you be given this contract, so that you may receive another one. It is a quick way for answered prayers as you put your trust in God.
6. Always pay the tithe for every contract won by you.

Chapter 30

FOR THOSE LOOKING UNTO GOD FOR MARITAL PARTNERS

Read: Gen. 24:1-14; 2:18 Ps. 32:8; Dan. 2:14-23, Ps. 138:8; 27:14, Isa. 40:31.
Sing: * Has God changed...
 * Do it, come and do it for me...

A lot of young people who are ripe for marriage are today walking about in frustration without a partner. This may be due to a lot of factors which may be physical or spiritual. Some have done everything physically possible but without success. This is the work of the enemy. You need a breakthrough, God did it in the past and He is still doing it, He will do it for you.

PRAY THESE PRAYERS:
1. Praise your creator first. Confess your sins and give Him thanks for all He has done in times past.
2. Father, you sent me into the world, I need my own partner according to your word in *Gen. 2:18*, give it to me today, in Jesus' name *(Three times)*.
3. Every fruit and seed of obstacles towards securing my own partner; be consumed by fire now, in Jesus' name *(Three times)*.
4. The mark of the enemy on me that is driving away my partner from me, be removed now by the blood of Jesus, in Jesus' name.
5. All walls of Jericho between me and the person God has chosen for me as partner begin to fall and sink, in Jesus' name *(Seven times)*.
6. Every curse of disappointment fighting against me over my marital life, I destroyed you by the power in the blood of Jesus, in Jesus' name *(Seven times)*.
7. I command every purpose and counsel of the enemy against me

not to get God's chosen partner, to be destroyed now, in Jesus' name.
8. O Lord, let the favour of God that makes one to know how to get the right marital partner, cover me now from head to toe, in Jesus' name.
9. Every Red Sea that separates me from my marital success in life, part now into two for me to go, in Jesus' name.
10. From now, I am progressing, my joy has come, and I receive it, in Jesus' name.
11. I loose my marital partner and myself from wherever we have been tied in order not to meet each other and I command the Holy Spirit to bring us together, in Jesus' name (Seven times).
12. Oh, Lord my God, the Creator of heaven and earth, the provider of all things, I thank you for your unfailing mercy and truth towards me. You have made everything good in my time. You have provided a good husband *(or wife)* for me in fulfilment of your word upon me, to be fruitful and multiply.
13. You that provided a good wife for Isaac the son of Abraham You will not but provide a good *(wife)* husband for me this year. This is because I am confident that you will perfect those things, which concerns me. Lord, your mercy endures forever; forsake not the work of thy hand in Jesus' name.
14. Let the wall of hindrance that separates me from my future partner fall right now, in Jesus name.

Give thanks to God because your marital partner has come. Open your spiritual eyes and see with the natural ones. Be expectant now. Be careful of satanic deceit. Pray very well and spiritually examine whoever comes via his faith, family and work. Seek counsel from a mature man or woman of God. Pray very well before giving out your Yes, I do.

Sing: * *God will make a way...*

Chapter **31**

WHEN YOUR CHILD IS STUBBORN AND DISOBEDIENT

Read: *Isaiah 8:18, Ps 127, Ps 128:3b, Pro 23:2, Isa. 54:13,*
I Thess 5:5, Luke 2:2:51-52, Pr 21:1.

Sing: ** All I have is given to me by my Lord...*
(Mention your child's name) is given to me by Jesus.

Disobedience or stubbornness is a demon that troubles many children today, disturbing the peace of homes and putting shame on parents. To overcome this, parents must declare a total spiritual war against this demon. This can only be done by the power of God, through prayers. So with fasting, pray this prayer in faith for the total deliverance of the child. God will do it again.

PRAY THESE PRAYERS:
1. Plead the blood of Jesus on the child for *(two minutes).*
2. I release the fire and power of God on (...)* in Jesus' name.
3. Every demon in the life of (...),* I command you to loose your grip and come out, in Jesus' name.
4. You spirit of stubbornness, I release the fire of God on you now, pack out your load and go, in Jesus' name.
5. Every spirit that works contrary to the commandment and laws of God begin to come out of (...)* and go into the sea now, in Jesus' name.
6. Holy Spirit, begin to purge the heart of (...)* with the blood of Jesus and your fire in Jesus' name.
7. I call the fire of God to burn the bond and every demon that has put (...)* in bondage, in Jesus' name.
8. Every familiar spirits possessing (...)* I bind you all and cast you into the sea, in Jesus' name.

For Victory and Abundant Blessings in all life s situations

9. Lord, the heart of (...)* is in your hand, turn it in your mercy according to your good will, in Jesus' name.
10. Lord, anyone that wishes to use my child to trouble my life, put him or her into life bondage, in Jesus' name.
11. God, you gave me this child to be a blessing and not a curse to me, so shall it be from now on, in Jesus' name.
12. (...)* Will not die, he (she) will live to proclaim the name of the Lord Jesus, in Jesus' name.
13. (...)* you will be a kind and peaceful child, in Jesus' name. My labour on (...) will not be in vain, I will surely enjoy the fruit of my labour on (...)*, in Jesus' name.

WHAT TO DO:

· Make sure you show love and care to that child. Do not curse or use any bad words against him or her.
· Present the gospel of Jesus to him or her in love and pray every day for him with fasting. Pray together with him or her as the situation permits.
· Have faith in God and believe that the Lord will deliver the child. Always look at the child as your loving son or daughter that will be great in future. Rejoice in the Lord and always praise the Lord for him or her. Victory is yours.

Sing: The Lord has given me victory; I will lift Him higher...

For Victory and Abundant Blessings in all life's situations

Chapter 32

VICTORY OVER WRONG ACCUSATION AND COURT CASES

Read: Ps. 26, Isa. 50:4-1, Matt. 5:25, Luke. 18:1-18.
Sing: * O that men would praise the Lord...

A lot of people have found themselves in the net of crimes they don't know anything about. The Yoruba people always pray that: may we never get entangled in other people's cases and troubles. Although, this is a good prayer, but the precaution you need to take is to pray ahead of time.

PRAY THESE PRAYERS:
1. Praise God heartily, confess your sins and thank Him for all His goodness over your life.
2. My God, deliver me from the spirit behind getting robed in another man's trouble today, in Jesus' name.
3. Every plan of the enemy to drag me into any case I don't know anything about, I destroy by the power in the blood of Jesus, in Jesus' name.
4. My Lord, raise up people like Gamaliel in the Bible for my defence concerning this case, in Jesus' name.
5. Every curse tending towards entanglement with court case and trouble is removed today from my life by the power in the blood of Jesus.
6. The enemy robbing me up with courts cases, seeking troubles for me, Father, let the stone of affliction that will make him forget about me be thrown into his life in Jesus' name.
7. Host of heaven, clear away all enemies, their court cases and troubles from my life, in Jesus' name.
8. Every sign of case and trouble entanglement that the enemy has put

on me, Lord, blot them off by the blood of Jesus.
9. Holy Spirit, deliver me completely from the yoke of court cases today and intervene in this case, in Jesus' name.
10. My Lord, you are the Prince of Peace, grant me peace in all my ways, in Jesus' name.
11. Holy Ghost, give me rest of mind from this or any trouble, in Jesus' name.
12. I reject being imprisoned, in Jesus' name *(Seven times)*.
13. I declare total liberation upon myself, in Jesus' name *(Seven times)*.
Cover yourself with the blood of Jesus as you go to where the case is to be heard, and be talking to the heavenly advocate to consider your matter. Make sure that you always use the word of God as it comes in to your heart. The Word of God will surely give you peace of mind as you meditate on what God had done before and what He can do now. Come on, relax, Jesus is in control of the case. Trust in Him and sing unto His praise on what you want Him to do in this matter.

Sing: * *Forever O! Lord, the word…*

Chapter 33

PRAYER OF VICTORY OVER FLESH

Read: *Ps. 51; Jn. 6:63; Rom. 8:11*
Sing: ** Into my heart...*
* My body is your Sanctuary...

When you are going into some sins that have become habits due to the demand of the flesh e.g. sexual immorality, lust, anger and so on. You have tried to leave them but you find it impossible. Then you have to talk to God about it. The prayers below will definitely help you out.

PRAY THESE PRAYERS:

1. O Lord, take dominion over the flesh that tempts me to sin against you, in Jesus' name.
2. Today, Lord, destroy from me every battle that has given me bad name, in Jesus' name.
3. Every sin of the flesh that fights me secretly and openly, Holy Spirit remove it today, in Jesus' name.
4. O Jehovah, destroy today, every carnal behaviour inherited from my parents, in Jesus' name.
5. Lord, all the desires of the flesh that are causing setbacks in my life making me backward among my peers, destroy them in Jesus name.
6. Holy Spirit, the flesh is about to make me fall, uphold me, in Jesus name (Seven times).
7. Holy Spirit, by your authority, I overcome the devil, sin and world from today, in Jesus' name (Seven times).
8. Place your right hand on your head or chest and raise the left up call the name of Jesus three times with great zeal, and say: Lord make me victorious over flesh, in Jesus' name.

- For Victory and Abundant Blessings in all life's situations

9. No matter how the case may be, Lord help me and strengthen me in this Christian race, in Jesus' name.
10. Lord, fill me with righteousness and joy, in the name of Jesus.
11. Holy Ghost, help me to be able to lay aside every weight and sin which easily beset me, in Jesus' name.
12. Lord, put a wall of separation between me and every spirit of idolatry operating in my life, in any form it might take, in Jesus' name.
13. Holy Ghost, take total control of my life from today, in Jesus' name.
14. Lord, uproot every seed of the enemy and change the heart of stone in my life, in Jesus' name.
15. Holy Ghost fire, come down and consume every garbage in my life, in Jesus' name.
16. I receive fresh favour from the Lord, in Jesus' name.
17. I enter into covenant of success with God for success in every area of my life, in Jesus' name.
18. Flesh, I have dominion over you today, in Jesus' name.
19. I shall not fall, in Jesus' name.
    Run away from every form of temptation and you shall not sin.

Sing: *I am going higher yes I am...*

For Victory and Abundant Blessings in all life's situations

Chapter 34

PERSONAL DELIVERANCE

Read: Obadiah 17; Jn. 8:32; Rom. 8:2; II Cor.3: 17; Isa. 9:4; Lk.10: 19; Rev. 12:11; I Jn. 4:4.

Sing: * I plead the blood, the blood of Jesus...
* O! The blood of Jesus...

Deliverance is not something you do once and forget it altogether. It is to be done repeatedly and at regular intervals. If you have a bad dream either in the day or at night, rise up and take the steps you will find below: If everything seems mixed up for you, following all these steps will help you a lot. Decide to be delivered. Also, believe that God will deliver you. There are three principal weapons of warfare you can use: They are the Blood of Jesus, the Word of God and the Name of Jesus. In the Blood, we have the redemption and even the forgiveness of sins – *Colosians1: 14*. The Word of God is the Sword of the Spirit – *Ephesians 6: 17*. At the name of Jesus, every knee shall bow – *Philippians 2; 9-11*.

NOW TAKE THESE STEPS:

1. Begin to call the blood of Jesus over your house and compound for about three minutes
2. Call Holy Ghost fire to surround the house and compound for about three minutes. Begin to send all the evil spirits in your vicinity to the Red Sea and bind them there in Jesus' name.
3. Now, stand or sit properly, place your right or left finger on your navel, put the other hand at your mouth as if to drink and begin to drink the blood of Jesus. Say **"I drink the blood of Jesus"** for about ten minutes. In the spirit, envision the blood of Jesus as it is passing through your mouth into your gullet, your chest and stomach.

■ For Victory and Abundant Blessings in all life's situations

New Breakthrough Prayers

4. After this, begin to command all the evil spirits troubling you to get out and go into the sea. Use ample time to send them out one after the other. Call them by their names. Do it for at least five minutes. Do it again and do it the third time. Do not be afraid peradventure you are about vomiting. Pour it out do not swallow it. If you are yawning or belching or releasing anal gas, those evil spirits are going out, let them go out.

5. Drink the blood of Jesus for about five minutes; put your hand in your mouth as if you are drinking with your hand from the tap, the other hand on your navel. Vomit if you want to vomit, belch if you want to belch, release the gas if you feel like, fear not, let them go out.

6. Begin to cancel all evil covenants in your life. The ones you entered into before you were born or that which was made with you through blood, word, cloth, candle and spiritual bath in the river and so on, in the name of Jesus.

7. Have you taken your cloth to an herbalist before or have you been bathed in the river? Have you prayed or been prayed for with candle before or incisions have been made on you or things like that? Use the blood of Jesus to cancel every demonic thing you know in your life *(Col. 2:4)* if not, true deliverance will not happen. Call the blood of Jesus vigorously several times. Also, use the blood of Jesus to cancel all past covenants ignorantly made by your confession, in Jesus' name *(Matt. 12:37)*.

8. Call the Holy Ghost fire to surround you and destroy every spirit behind evil covenant or the work of the devil in your life or house, buried or hung on the wall or blown into the air over your life issue.

9. Call the thunder of heaven to scatter the entire spiritual mirror by which the enemy views and monitor the issue of your life, in Jesus' name. Also, command the spiritual cord binding you and evil covenants, curse or any bondage, let all be broken right now.

10. Now, ask the Holy Spirit to fill your life and enter your heart. Say this for about three minutes. Make confession that your bondage is broken; sing it and give thanks to the creator.

| 79 |

11. Believe that Jesus has set you free. Henceforth, run from sins, pray always, be preoccupied with the Word of God, go to church regularly and let praises unto God fill your heart at all times.

Sing: ** I am delivered, Praise the Lord...*
* You are worthy O! Lord...

Chapter 35

WAGING WAR AGAINST SEPARATION AND DIVORCE IN MARRIAGE

Read: Gen. 2:18, Matt. 19:6 Mat. 2:13-16.
Sing: *You are the mighty God, the great I am...*

Separation and divorce are spirit of the devil, not from God. The plan of God is for the wife and husband to stay together in love till death do them apart. So, stand against the spirit of separation and divorce now!

Sing: *Victory, victory hallelujah...*

PRAY THESE PRAYERS:
1. In Jesus' name, I confront all the powers of the devil confronting my family and causing marital crisis with the fire of the Holy Ghost.
2. I command the spirit of wandering operating in the life of my husband (or wife) to disappear, in Jesus' name.
3. All the powers of Satan directed against my family is destroyed, in Jesus' name (Three times).
4. I pursue, overtake and retrieve my marriage from the hands of home destroyers, in Jesus' name (Three times).
5. All demonic weapons of war and anger against my family, be consumed completely, in Jesus' name (Three times).
6. I snatch my husband (wife) from those who tempt one to commit evil, in Jesus' name.
7. Let every suggestion, thought, decision, plan, counsel and hope of divorce and separation in my family be nullified, in Jesus' name (Three times).
8. Every evil bird pecking up my love in the heart of my husband, (or wife) (...), be burnt up, in Jesus' name.
9. I refuse to be the second wife or husband or a single woman or man

(mention the one applicable to you), in Jesus' name.
10. I break every bondage of polygamy from the life of my husband, in Jesus' name.
11. I snatch my husband *(wife)* from strange women *(men)* who plunder men's (women's) substances, in Jesus' name (Seven times).
12. I cut every spirit binding my husband *(wife)* and (...) *(mention the name of the strange woman (man) if you know it)* with the axe of God, in Jesus' name *(Dramatise it) (Seven times)*.
13. I destroy every sign of hatred and anger troubling my home, in Jesus' name.
14. I decree disappointment, affliction and shame on unlawful relationship between my husband *(wife)* and any strange woman *(man)*, in Jesus' name.
15. Thank God for the answered prayers.

I implore you strongly to behave in such ways as would attract your husband or wife to you. Let your home be at peace for either him or her to desire to come home on time. Do not let your home be in turmoil. Be affectionate to him or her; also take care of him or her in love. Respect him or her as you ought to. GOD will uphold your home in Jesus Christ's name. Amen. After all these, then, wait upon God and see the glory of God – Ps 27:14, Ex14.

Sing: * *God is good; He has done me well, oh my soul...*

For Victory and Abundant Blessings in all life's situations

Chapter 36

PRAYER FOR SPECIAL GOODNESS

Read: *Ps. 34: 1-10; 23:1-6*
Sing: ** I am serving a God of miracle I know...*

Special goodness is something that every man needs to have in order to get to the fulfilment of his dream in life. It is a lifter that lifts from mediocrity to relevance. You need it in order to be able to reach your goal in life. Therefore, you have to pray for its release from God. It is only God that gives it.

Sing: ** Surely goodness and mercy shall follow me...*
* Let the spirit of the Lord come down...

PRAY THESE PRAYERS:

1. Father, connect me with important people who will help in bringing your goodness into my life from today, in Jesus' name.
2. Father, rub on me the sweet smelling perfume of Christ so that as from today, goodness and helpers will be looking for me, in Jesus' name.
3. Holy Spirit, I enter into your favour today. Let your oil of mercy falls on my head. Everywhere I go, let there be a way for me. Whatever I lay my hands upon; let it prosper, in Jesus' name.
4. I refuse to be stagnant again. I begin to progress from this time on. I receive promotion to the post I desire, in my life in Jesus' name.
5. All arrows of disappointment and retrogression confronting my life, I send you back to the senders seven times, in Jesus' name.
6. Father, from today, make it impossible for anyone to stand contrary to any good thing that I am starting, in Jesus' name.
7. From today, I receive divine mercy over all my applications and

| 83 |

interviews and other things I am in need of, in Jesus' name.

8. I decree that all who would hate me or wage war against my progress will never have rest to plot against me, in Jesus' name.
9. Lord, in the company of every gathering working against my future, plant a Gamaliel to speak for me *(Acts 5:33-40)*.
10. All you spirits of rejection and hatred, get out of my life now. Lord, let your Spirit anoint me for mercy now. Let goodness and mercy follow me from now on, in Jesus' name.
11. I receive your favour and that of good people everywhere I go. Your word says if my ways please you, you will make my enemies to be at peace with me. Whoever deliberately opposes my progress, I ask the Lord to give such one, the spirit of repentance. I bind the spirit that goes to oppose me, in Jesus' name. All, who refuse to be at peace with me and are bent on my downfall, let peace be far from them. Let their plans be shattered and let the afflictions of God be upon them, in Jesus' name.
12. From now on, through the name of Jesus and the blood of God's lamb, Lord, single me out for mercy, promotion, admission, employment, free education, visas to overseas countries and praises at all times. *(Three times)*.

I thank you Lord for using the blood of Jesus to cleanse my life and body from demonic stigma, marks and emblems of disappointment and rejection, in Jesus' name. Begin to worship God as you are led; praise Him several times for He is good and His mercies endure forever.

Chapter 37

VICTORY OVER ALL SPIRITS OF IMPOSSIBILITY

Read: Luke. 1:37; Mk. 9:23; Phil. 4:13; Isa. 58:11; Isa. 65: 1-23.
Sing: * I have a Father, who will never fail me...
* Has God change, my Lord will never change...

You have attempted a particular good thing which should have contributed to your progress over and over and it seems impossible. Sometimes, you moved closer to success before things blocked again. You can pray over it today for an outright breakthrough.

PRAY THESE PRAYERS:
1. Father, let all fruits and roots of impossibility in my life be uprooted and destroyed today, in Jesus' name.
2. I sweep away all the curses of impossibilities in my life and family, in the name of Jesus Christ.
3. I nullify every spirit and power of impossibilities in my life, in Jesus' name.
4. I am a child of God and nothing is impossible for my Father, therefore, every good thing I lay my hands on shall prosper today and forever, in Jesus' name.
6. The Lord is the power and strength of my life; therefore, I shall prosper and give glory to God in all my ways, in Jesus' name.
7. I (............)* shall have breakthrough, in Jesus' name.
8. I come against you spirit of impossibility, lose your hands from my work and family. I receive restoration in ten folds; I receive my fortunes back, in Jesus' name.

Begin to praise the name of the Lord for the victory.

Sing: Forever O Lord, thy word is settled in heaven...

Chapter 38

SUNDAY, SUNDAY PRAYER TABLETS

Read: Ps 31:15, Ecc. 3: 18, 9:12, Dan.2: 21, Matt.16: 3, Ps.19: 1-2,121:6, Eph.5: 6.
Sing: Oh Lord my God when...

Don't wait till you have a particular problem before you pray. You can pray so that you will not pray. This is the reason why this attitude of consistent praying is organised here for every week. You can also use it for each day, month or year. You don't have to wait till evil days before you pray.

PRAY THESE PRAYERS:

1. Now, O Lord as David cried unto you, I do likewise today and say *"my times are in your hands, deliver me from all enemies and from those who persecute me" (Ps, 31;15).*
2. O Lord, redeem my times and seasons from the hands of my enemies this week, in Jesus' name.
3. From now on, I command all the weapons of the devil being used to monitor my times and my life in the past to be destroyed, in Jesus' name.
4. Now, I remove my name from the calendar of the devil today, in Jesus' name.
5. In Jesus' name, I reverse whatever my enemy has programmed into the sun, moon and other heavenly bodies against my life; I destroy them all by the power, in the blood of Jesus.
6. Today, every evil thing that has been said and done against me in the heavenly places I turn them around for good, in Jesus' name.
7. I destroy whatever the enemy has programmed this week against my life and family, in Jesus' name.

| 86 |

* For Victory and Abundant Blessings in all life's situations

8. This week is my week, yes; it is my time and my turn to prosper. I appropriate into my life, all the blessings that God the creator of times and seasons has planned for this week, in Jesus' name.
9. I decree that all altars that have waged war against my life be shattered, in Jesus' name.
10. I prophesy this week, that you sun shall not smite me by day nor you moon by night, in Jesus' name.
11. I use the blood of Jesus to wash away all the evil inscriptions that have been written on my life and I destroy all the instruments being used by the enemy against my life, in Jesus' name.
12. I stop all satanic princes that are speaking to the sun, moon, stars and air concerning my life; I cause confusion in your kingdom and I destroy your plan, in Jesus' name.
13. Because the Bible says the days are evil, I therefore redeem this week from disasters, afflictions, failure and death by the blood of Jesus, in Jesus' name.
14. I programme the purpose and plan of God into the sun at this time and I decree that all the creatures of God begin to speak of God's glory concerning my family, and my work throughout this week, in Jesus' name.

Sing: * *I am serving a God of miracle I know...*
        * *Pray fervently and you will see the hand of God...*

Chapter **39**

VICTORY OVER DIVERSE DISEASES AND SICKNESS

Read: *Ps. 6:1-10; Jer. 17:14; Isa. 53:5, Matt 12:22; 9:20-22;*
Mk. 5:1-20; 9:14-27; Matt. 12:15.
Sing: ** Lord I lift your name on high...*

Disease and sickness' in the life or a man, is just like bile in the pot of joy. Many people who would have had a joyful and happy life have been thrown into the darkness of disease and sickness making life to be bitter for them. If you are one of such people, there is still Balm in Gilead. First turn to God, repent from all sin, check your life for any unconfessed sin and ask for forgiveness. Also, you have to know the sickness you are suffering from and where it is in your body, place your hand on the spot as you pray.

Sing: ** There is power mighty in the blood...*

PRAY THESE PRAYERS:
Call the blood of Jesus for a long time and pray these prayers several times:

1. My God, heal me from this sickness; give me victory over this disease, in Jesus' name.
2. My God, deliver me from the sickness of (...)* today, in Jesus' name
3. All you diseases rioting in my body, I command you to leave me now and get out, in Jesus' name.
4. You (...)*, you are a tree that my Father in heaven had not planted in my body; therefore, I uproot you now, in Jesus' name.
5. Call the blood of Jesus twenty-one times and pray: You this sickness that is called (...)*, the Lord rebukes you. Get out of your hidden places in my body, in Jesus' name.

For Victory and Abundant Blessings in all life s situations

6. Holy Ghost fire, begin to burn in my body now, in Jesus' name (pray this prayer for two minutes).
7. Call the blood of Jesus for about two minutes. Pray that, just as the fish have no discomfort in the water, Lord, put comfort in my body now, in Jesus' name.
8. Begin to confess that *"... by his stripes I am healed"* (Isa. 53:5), do this for about five minutes.
9. I receive my healing, in Jesus' name.

Begin to thank God with praise songs. Believe a miracle had happened to you now. Confess these words:

CONFESSION:
Because the word of God says it is the LORD Himself that heals me, I receive my healing today. Jesus Himself, has borne my grief, and carried my sorrows... and by His stripes I am healed. Therefore, you sickness that is afflicting me, I command you in the name of Jesus of Nazareth... come out *(do it for about five minutes every three-three hours, do not cease to confess Mathew 8:17 and I Peter 2: 24 until the symptoms of sickness depart from you completely)*. Remember that the word of God is quick *(i.e. alive)* and powerful – Heb.4: 12.

Sing: * *You are the Lord that healeth me...*

| 89 |

Chapter 40

PRAYER OF DELIVERANCE FROM ALL AFFLICTIONS

Read: Joshua 1:8, II Tim 4: 18, Jn 16:33
Sing: * O Lord! I am very, very grateful...

Afflictions are from the devil through his agents. There are different areas today by which people are afflicted. It may be due to curses that are generational or self inflicted or other sins apart from these. The result of every affliction is suffering, retardation, stagnancy, failure, frustration and many times untimely death. In order for the devil not to mortgage your destiny, you have to talk to God.

Sing: * In Jesus name every knee shall bow...

PRAY THESE PRAYERS:
1. Father, do not let me suffer for another man's sins, deliver me from all afflictions that my ancestors have brought into my life, in Jesus' name.
2. O Lord! remove every source of afflictions from my life. and rescue me from the spirit of servitude as from today, in Jesus' name.
3. Save me, O Lord! from the punishment of sins, curses and shame, in Jesus' name.
4. Lord, I reject pains and suffering, and I shall not be a servant to my mates, in Jesus' name.
5. O God! give me the authority of comfort with which I shall do all things to the glory of your name alone, in Jesus' name.
6. My God, give me the authority of comfort by which I shall be praying and speaking to you and overcome all the afflictions in my life, in Jesus' name.
7. My God, make me a person on whom your favour will shine today,

prosper me and make affliction a thing of the past in my life, in Jesus' name *(II Sam. 9)*.

8. The covenant of victory that God has made with me, Holy Spirit, let it manifest, in Jesus' name *(Ps. 89:34)*.

9. Where I think there is no way in my life, O my God! let there be way for me, in Jesus' name *(Ex. 14)*.

10. Holy Spirit, take afflictions away from my life, let your miracles start flowing like river into my life, in Jesus' name.

11. Lord, perform miracles that are older than my age and bigger than my position, that I may glorify you with the beloved. Let afflictions completely bid me farewell, in Jesus' name.

12. All my belongings that the enemy has stolen thereby causing afflictions in my life, Lord, restore them back to me, in Jesus' name.

13. My Lord, give me the key to my house, joy, goodness and wealth from now, in Jesus' name.

14. Every cry of insufficiency in my life, I command you to come to an end, in Jesus' name.

15. Lord, let me be healed and freed from the dungeon of this affliction that the enemy has put me into, in Jesus' name.

16. Lord, deliver me from confusion of mind as from today, in Jesus' name.

17. It is my turn to receive your goodness, O my God! Do miracles for me quickly that enemies may stop mocking at your name in my life, in Jesus' name.

18. My head and legs, deliberate over the affairs of my life, take me out of these afflictions and take me to the place of my miracles, in Jesus' name,

19. I become a conqueror today, in Jesus' name.

Begin to thank God and sing:

Sing: * ***What manner of man is Jesus...***

Chapter 41

DAILY PRAYERS ON OPEN DOORS FOR DIVINE BLESSINGS

Read: *Job 31:32, Matt. 7:7; II Cor. 2:12; Isa. 43:18-19, Rev. 3:7*
Sing: ** Do something new in my life...*

Today, many people are struggling with the door of their success and breakthrough just because the enemy had denied them access through it. Even though, God has prepared it, the devil has denied it. It is high time you stop struggling with the door of success. Come to Him that has the key of David, He that opens and no man is able to shut, He that shuts and no man is able to open, Jesus Christ the Lord. He will save you and you shall glorify Him.

PRAY THESE PRAYERS:

1. Sudden goodness, unexpected miracle, ready-made blessings, Lord, direct them to me, in Jesus' name.
2. Every food and water of adversity, Lord, remove from my mouth, in Jesus' name.
3. Wherever the enemy has locked my benefactor, Lord, release him quickly that he may show kindness to me, in Jesus' name.
4. Among so many people, Father, let my miracle be possible, in Jesus' name.
5. Lord, do not let the blessing of my early life be carried over to the intermediate stage of life, do not let that of my intermediate stage be postponed to the latter part of my life and that of my latter life be carried into the grave. Bless me at the right time; this is the right time bless me O Lord! in Jesus' name.
6. As rivulet *(small stream)* locates the river, let my divine blessing find me out, in Jesus' name.
7. Lord, let the path to my goodness be opened today, in Jesus' name.

■ For Victory and Abundant Blessings in all life's situations

8. Every blessing that befits a child of God, Lord, give to me today, in Jesus' name.
9. O Lord! let the inheritance of righteousness be my portion today, in Jesus' name.
10. My God, do a new miracle in my life today and let it manifest, in Jesus' name.
11. The miracle that will make me to forget the problems of the past let it happen in my life today, in Jesus' name.
12. Let my own goodness in this life come unto me O Lord. Do not let me waste my life-time any longer, in Jesus' name.
13. Today, I reclaim every blessing that the enemy has robbed me of, in Jesus' name.
14. Lord, take control of the journey of my life today. Direct my footstep, lead me to the right place that I may come back with abundant goodness and blessings, in Jesus' name.
15. Lord, let me live my life in peace and abundant wealth, in Jesus' name.
16. Lord, let the thirst for holy life and the expectation of Christ's return; dwell in me, every minute of this day, in Jesus' name.

Begin to thank God, give Him a high praise.

Sing: Lord I lift your name on high...

| 93 |

Chapter 42

PRAYER FOR DIVINE HELP IN BUSINESS OR CAREER

Read: Ps.121; Heb.1:14, Ps. 23, Ps.138: 8
Sing: * There shall be showers of blessing...

The Bible says whoever does not work should not eat. Work, therefore, to live to the glory of God. But even after yielding to the above biblical injunction, you still need help from God for success and breakthrough. It takes help from God in form of grace, favour and mercy, for a man to be successful in his work or business.

PRAY THESE PRAYERS:
1. Lord, raise help for me in my work, with your mighty hand, that I may become great to the glory of your name, in Jesus' name.
2. My God, use the help of my co-workers to make this business great, in Jesus' name.
3. Lord, use the help of friends to uplift my work, in Jesus' name.
4. Holy Spirit, use my work to positively surprise and bless me to your glory alone, in Jesus' name.
5. My God, enlarge my work and perfect it to your praise alone, in Jesus' name.
6. Lord, keep my work under your merciful eyes, in Jesus' name.
7. Lord, help me and establish me fully and make way for me in this land and in this country. Lord, let the fame of my work spread all over, and make it my Rehoboth, in Jesus' name.
8. Lord, uphold my work with your mighty hand. Do not allow the enemy to destroy my work, in Jesus' name.
9. When Satan departed from Jesus, the Bible says, angels came to minister to Him. Today, I, an heir of salvation, command you, my angel, and you holy angels of God, the Lord of Hosts, to go forth

and compel customers and other purchasers of my merchandise to come right now. It is imperative for you angels of God to do this my bidding because the scriptures say that you all are ministering spirits who have been sent to minister to them who shall be heirs of salvation. Do this in Jesus name.

10. Just as you ministered to Jesus my Lord when He was in the flesh, so also must you angels of God go forth to minister in order to help me in all ways today, in Jesus name.

11. Just as you caused the raven to unfailingly bring bread and meat to Elijah morning and evening at the brook of Cherith beyond Jordan, so must you bring customers, purchasers for my goods both morning and all the day long, in Jesus name.

12. I command you angels of the Lord to go forth quickly and bring customers in for me to come and purchase these goods that I am touching, and cause them also to pay immediately for them. Because the Lord is my shepherd I will not lack credible customers both male and female today. The reason why my goods must sell well today is that I also pay my tithes and offerings regularly.

Sing: * *Thank you Jesus, the owner of my soul,*
         * *Alpha Omega, you are worthy to be praised...*

Chapter **43**

DAILY DEMANDING FOR ONE'S RIGHTS

Read: **Ps. 118:24**
Sing: ** Holy Ghost, do it again, do it again in my life...*
* This is the day that the Lord has made...

For the people of God, there are benefits provided each day for them by God Himself. The Bible says, He daily loads His people with benefits. Why then are you still suffering? You have to tap into the mainstream of the benefits of God the Father today for a joyful and glorious life. But are you born again? Have you given your life to Jesus? For all that pertains to life is in Jesus. You receive it today, by repenting and forsaking your sins and following Jesus. He will bless you.

Sing: * All I have, they are given to me by the Lord...

PRAY THESE PRAYERS:
1. I confess that this is the day that the Lord has made, therefore, joy, goodness and blessings are mine, in Jesus' name.
2. Evil luck that the enemy could have put in the beginning, middle and the end of *(day, week, month, year),* Lord, let it not be my portion and that of my family, in Jesus' name.
3. In this year, month, week or day, I shall not lose my child, wife or husband or work, in Jesus' name.
4. Lord, I reject from my life and family, all daily, monthly or yearly disasters and troubles that move all around, in Jesus' name.
5. Lord, let there be allowance for me anywhere I get to today, this week, month or year, in Jesus' name.
6. That gift that you have deposited in my body, O God! let it not be of ridicule in the hands of my enemies, in Jesus' name.

| 96 |

For Victory and Abundant Blessings in all life's situations

7. Jesus, mediate between God and me today because of your blood.
8. All spiritual and physical thieves, Lord, give them no chance in my life, in Jesus' name.
9. I sanctify everything that belongs to me with the blood of Jesus, in Jesus' name.
10. Lord, plant in my life, the power of victory over enemies.
11. Turn me to fire and sun in the presence of my enemies, in Jesus' name.
12. I want to be great in faith, Lord Jesus, lift my hands up spiritually and physically this year, in Jesus' name.
13. My God, do not let me fall into the trap of my enemy today, in Jesus' name.
14. My Lords, make me partaker of all the blessings of this day, week, month and year. Use good people to bless me in all ways, in Jesus' name.
15. My Lord, from today, grant me your wisdom, understanding, knowledge, in Jesus' name.
16. Holy Spirit the comforter, help me today, in all my undertakings, in Jesus' name.
17. Eastern winds, as you brought food for the Israelites in the wilderness in those days, bring my goodness to me, in Jesus' name.

Your right as a child is that it should be well with you (3 John 2), therefore claim and hold on to it.

Sing: ** My lifetime, I will give all my lifetime...*
* Connection, connection o...

Chapter 44

SPECIAL PRAYER FOR TORMENTORS

Read: Revelation 12: 11, Psalm 27.
Sing: * Anywhere enemies are gather,
  * Holy Ghost fire consume them...

The Bible confirms it that it is evil that will kill the wicked. So, are you under the battle of tormentors? Are you being afflicted daily by the enemy? Fire back with the arrow of God and destroy through Holy Ghost fire the bondage of the enemies for a total deliverance.

PRAY THESE PRAYERS

1. You arrow of the Lord! to wherever the tormentors are gathered because of me, scatter them, in Jesus' name.
2. All enemies appearing to me as friends, Lord, expose their secrets where no one will cover them, in Jesus' name.
3. You sword of the Lord! I command you to visit all who have covenanted with the darkness in order to harm me, in Jesus' name.
4. All who are afflicting me, Lord, afflict them today, in Jesus' name.
5. Call Holy Ghost fire once and say: All that are tormenting me because of your glory upon my life, fire of heaven begin to burn them, in Jesus' name.
6. Pray this prayer with your right hand lifted up: O thunder of God! Strike with a terrible loud noise, let there be a terrible loud crying and weeping in the house of whoever wishes my family and me dead, in Jesus' name.
7. Call the name of Jesus once and say: O Lord!, anyone born or taken out of a woman who says there shall be no way for me, afflict him or her with a terrible trouble so much so that he will not even have time for my own affairs any longer, in Jesus' name.

Chapter 45

PRAYER FOR GOD'S GENERAL PROTECTION

Read: Ps. 121, Ps. 27, and Ps.37
Sing: Rock of ages, cleft for me...

The Lord has promised that, He will set your feet on the road you walk and with His eyes He shall go with you. Many have been walking alone in the journey of life and the outcome has been sorrow and affliction from the enemies. You cannot walk alone in life journey. If you walk alone you will die alone. You need the protection and mercy of God. Why not come to Him today and enjoy His presence.

PRAY THESE PRAYERS:
1. Call the name of Jesus once with great zeal and say: LET THE hand of God protect me and everything I have from the fire of the enemies, in Jesus' name.
2. Call the name of Jesus seven times and say: The journey I will undertake that I will not return this year, Lord, do not let me embark on it, in Jesus' name.
3. Call the name of Jesus three times and say: Holy Spirit put your hedge of protection around my family and me, in Jesus' name.
4. Place both hands on your head and call the name of Jesus three times and say: Lord, do not allow what will make me lament in sorrow to happen to me this year, in Jesus' name.
5. Point your right hand on the ground, call the name of Jesus three times and say: O earth! earth!!, you will not swallow my family or me this year, in Jesus' name.
6. Call the name of Jesus once and say: Lord, because of your word, those who are after my life, exchange their lives for mine, according to your word in *Isaiah. 43:4*.

For Victory and Abundant Blessings in all life's situations

7. Place your right hand on the entrance to your house or room and call the name of Jesus, blood of Jesus and Holy Spirit, then say: I command that my house becomes Goshen – a place of protection from death and disease this year, in Jesus' name (Seven times).

Sing: *The steadfast love of the Lord...*

For Victory and Abundant Blessings in all life's situations

Chapter 46

GENERAL PRAYER POINTS FOR TOTAL RECOVERY AND GENERAL PURPOSES

Read: Heb.13:5, 1Sam.12:2, Isa.41:10, Deut.33:27,
Psalm 5, 57, 86, 121,130, 119: 169-176

Sing: *Do it come and do it for me...*

A lot of people stopped praying so early, just when their restoration and recovery have just started coming up. The devil has taken a lot of things from you, remember, you don't have to stop until you have taken back all that the enemy has taken. The Bible says, David pursued, overtook and recovered all that the enemy has taken. Has enemy take your job, wife, husband, child, property and so on. You can recover all and even add extra today through Christ Jesus.

PRAY THESE PRAYERS:

1. O Lord! I receive back the restoration of all that the enemies has taken away from me, in Jesus' name.
2. Lord, neutralise every occult power that my enemy relies on in harming me, in Jesus' name.
3. Lord, cleanse me from every evil mark that the enemy might have put upon me, in Jesus' name.
4. From all the oppressors of my life that had died, O Lord, take back for me my covenant rights and benefits, Father, cause them to restore it seven fold, in Jesus' name.
5. Lord, turn every channel of sorrow in my life to joy, in the name of Jesus.
6. Lord, open up every hidden glory in my life, in Jesus' name.
7. Father, cause me to have breakthrough in every aspect of my life before the end of this year, in Jesus' name.
8. Lord, grant unto me the spirit of perseverance in the place of prayer, in Jesus' name.

For Victory and Abundant Blessings in all life's situations •

9. Lord, open before me the door of success, in Jesus' name.
10. Lord, confuse those who have been standing against your will for my life, cause them to begin to fight themselves, in Jesus' name.
11. Holy Ghost, consume every power that turns original miracles to counterfeit in my life, in Jesus' name.
12. I release the fire of the Holy Ghost against those who pursue me, in Jesus' name.
13. Lord, you are the one that terminated the life of Saul in order for David to reign. Destroy anyone standing between me and my miracle, in Jesus' name.
14. Lord, destroy the garment of shame that the enemy has made for me, in Jesus' name.
15. No matter how the fire might spread, it cannot cross the river to the other side, do not allow the powers of the enemy to have impact upon me, in the name of Jesus.
16. Lord, smite my enemies with blindness, in Jesus' name.
17. Every mark that makes me stink to my helper is cleansed by the power in the blood of Jesus today in Jesus' name.
18. Lord, I command every strange spirits causing me to lose good things to quit now, in Jesus' name.
19. Lord, strangle every curse that is strangling my goodness, in the name of Jesus.
20. I abort every sad news the enemy is cooking up on my behalf, in Jesus' name.
21. Jesus, your blood is a divine eraser; cleanse me from every form of curse in my life, in Jesus' name.
22. Lord, point and direct me to my helper in Jesus' name.
23. Lord, let testimony be my portion, in Jesus' name.
24. Lord, I receive, the miracles that draw crowd, let it be my portion, in Jesus' name.
25. Salt is incomparable to any recipe in the kitchen, do not allow the enemy to substitute my rightful position to another person in my office, family or country, in Jesus' name.
26. Lord, grant unto me the unbelievable miracle of my life this month, in Jesus' name.

For Victory and Abundant Blessings in all life s situations

27. Lord, do not allow the enemy to make me a victim of their evil work in this world.
28. Lord, destroy the garment of poverty, affliction and shame from my life, in Jesus' name.
29. O Lord! visit with sudden death, every wolf putting on sheep's skin in order to seek after my life, in Jesus' name.
30. Lord, perform a mighty miracle that will make my enemy serve me, in Jesus' name
31. Lord, put all the enemies that make evil publication of me into bondage, in Jesus' name.
32. I bind and cast into fire the spirit of death threatening my life, in Jesus' name.
33. Lord, swallow up every power hindering my success, in Jesus' name.
34. Every root of residual spirits in my life be uprooted and consumed with fire, in Jesus' name.
35. Lord, put upon me the garment of success, in Jesus name.
36. Lord, before those who make me a laughing stock, make me a great man, in Jesus' name.
37. Lord, put the mark of favour upon me, in Jesus' name.
38. Lord, lift my head before my families, friends, companies and contemporaries, in Jesus' name.
39. You earth listen, I decree that you will not swallow up my wife, children, well-wishers and me, in Jesus' name.
40. Let all the dead people that might have carried away my glory begin to vomit them, in Jesus' name.
41. Lord, smite my enemies with thunderous blows, in Jesus' name.
42. Lord, divide the tongues of my enemies and put them in confusion, in Jesus' name.
43. Lord, carry me over all the walls of Jericho hindering my progress, in Jesus' name.
44. Lord, I rebuke every spirit of carelessness about my predicament, in Jesus' name.
45. I take authority over every spirit of doubt and unbelief in my life, in Jesus' name.

46. No matter what the economy of this nation looks like, I will make it, in Jesus' name.
47. Lord, open my eyes to every hidden problem in my life, in Jesus' name.
48. Lord, divinely connect me with my miracle, in Jesus' name.
49. Every stronghold of the devil in my life, be destroyed, in Jesus' name.
50. Lord, speak to me today, a word that will change my life, in Jesus' name.
51. Lord, I trust you for my desired success, in the name of Jesus.
52. Lord, let the spirit of righteousness and holiness possess me, in Jesus' name.
53. Father, let the spirit of boldness that inspires for exploits to the glory of God, possess me, in Jesus' name.
54. I receive the power of God to possess for my covenant rights, in Jesus' name.
55. Lord, whatsoever is hindering my way to Canaan, my land of fulfilment, overturn it, in Jesus name.
56. Lord, open my eyes to understand your divine purpose for me, in Jesus' name.
57. Lord, let the latter part of my life be better than the beginning, in Jesus' name.
58. Lord, quench the fire of curse that sin has brought into my life, in Jesus' name.
59. Lord, blot out all the demonic ordinances that were written against me, in Jesus' name.
60. No matter how the case may be, Lord, help me and strengthen me in this Christian race, in Jesus' name.
61. Lord, fill me with joy today, in the name of Jesus
62. Holy Ghost, help me to be able to lay aside every weight of sin that easily beset me, in Jesus' name.
63. Lord, put a wall of separation between me and every spirit of idolatry operating in my life in Jesus' name.
64. Holy Ghost, take total control of my life from today, in Jesus' name.

65. Lord, uproot every seed of evil and transform my heart of stone into flesh, in Jesus' name.
66. I receive fresh favour from the Lord, in Jesus' name.
67. I enter into eternal covenant with God for success, in Jesus' name.

New Breakthrough Prayers

For Victory and Abundant Blessings in all life's situations ■

Chapter **47**

PRAYER FOR THE BEREAVED

Read: *Job 8:20; Ps. 23; 63:1-8, Rm. 8:18-39, I Cor. 15:35-57, II Cor. 15:35-57, II Cor. 5:1-10, Jer. 31:15 II Tim. 1:8-10, Nahum 1:7-9*

Sing: ** Because He lives I can face tomorrow...*
* Let your living water flows of over my soul...

Situation and circumstance might have robbed you, of the life of a beloved relation, close associate or somebody that is dare to you which left you dejected and full of sorrow or even makes you to be thinking of dying or full of fear of death. Commit yourself to the hand of God for the comfort of your soul.

Sing: Take control Holy Spirit...

PRAY THESE PRAYERS:
1. Praise God for everything for five minutes.
2. Plead the blood of Jesus on yourself.
3. I surrender my body, soul and spirit into your hand Holy Spirit; take control, in Jesus' name.
4. Every door of sorrow and grief opened by the enemy, I close you, in Jesus' name.
5. I receive the comfort of the Holy Spirit, in Jesus' name
6. Shepherd of my soul, take control of my life now and let your peace flow over my soul, in Jesus' name.
7. Lord, let the spirit of sorrow packs its load and leave my life, in Jesus' name.
8. I bade goodbye to you today you demons of grief and heavy heart, in Jesus' name.

| 106 |

For Victory and Abundant Blessings in all life s situations

New Breakthrough Prayers

9. I rebuke you spirit of death from troubling me and from parading this environment, in Jesus' name.
10. Every power that bows down my head and subject my spirit to grief I bind you and send you away from my life, in Jesus' name.
11. I receive Joy instead of sorrow, in Jesus' name.
12. Lord Jesus, you are the comfort of the troubled soul, comfort me, in Jesus' name.
13. Every hand that has been feeding me with food of oppression, water of bitterness and sorrow, I destroy you with the fire of the Lord, in Jesus' name.
14. You thief of soul and spirit I put an end to all your activities in my home, in Jesus' name.
15. I command you my spirit to come back to a peaceful state, in Jesus' name.
16. According to Jabez, Lord I pray that I may never see evil again, all the days of my life, in Jesus' name.
17. My Joy that the enemy has stolen, I receive back, in Jesus' name.
18. The Bible says that David encouraged himself in Lord, therefore, I receive encouragement and strength from the Lord for my spirit, in Jesus' name.
19. Let the hand of the Lord; remove the garment of mourning from my life right now, in Jesus' name.
20. Father, send the miracle that will make me forget my sorrow from now, in Jesus' name.
21. I break the yoke of continuous sorrow from my life, in Jesus' name.
22. Let the hand of God, release my stolen joy from the hand of the enemy, in Jesus' name.

The Bible says rejoice, you don't have to mourn, put the sorrow of life away from you and receive the consolation of the Holy Spirit. It is well with you, in Jesus' name *(Philippians 4:4).*

Sing: Into my heart, come into my heart... (Several times)

New Breakthrough Prayers   For Victory and Abundant Blessings in all life's situations ■

Chapter **48**

PRAYER FOR
LONGEVITY

Read: Ps. 91:16
*Sing: * Thank you, thank you Lord...*
* * Thank you Jesus, the owner of my life...*

The Lord has promised to satisfy us with long life. So, long life is your inheritance, don't allow the enemy to cheat you, therefore, claim it today.

*Sing: * Thank you Jesus, the owner of my life...*

PRAY THESE PRAYERS:
1. Thank the Lord, for giving you life.
2. Thank the Lord, for your parents or guardians, through whom you were brought up.
3. Thank the Lord that the world has not rendered you useless in life.
4. Ask for forgiveness of sins.
5. Ask for Holy Spirit's sovereignty in your heart.
6. I erase the spirit of sudden death from my generation with the blood of Jesus, in Jesus' name.
7. Holy Spirit, destroy every thought and plan of the devil to cut-short my life, in Jesus' name.
8. Holy Spirit, destroy every form of sickness meant by the devil to cut-short my life, in Jesus' name.
9. Let every evil the enemy wishes me, boomerang on them, in the name of Jesus.
10. The sun never dawns at noon, my glory will never dawn at its prime, in Jesus' name.
11. No one sees the end of the sea; the enemy will not know the end of my life, in Jesus' name.

|108|

12. Create in me, a refreshing power that will sustain me all through life, in Jesus' name.
13. Every cell, tissue, organ and system in me receive an excellent spirit and a power that overcomes principalities and powers of darkness, in Jesus' name.
14. I refuse to be a reproach in life and I will not lack anything good, in Jesus' name.
15. I shall not die but live to declare the glory of the Lord, in Jesus' name.
16. Lord make my life and my time incomprehensible by the enemy, in the name of Jesus.
17. Holy Spirit, be my guide and teacher all through my life and satisfy me with long life and salvation.
18. You granted Methuselah the grace to live long, Lord; I receive the grace to live to an old age.
19. I shall not plant for another man to harvest, nor labour for another man to reap; I receive long life to enjoy all my labour in life, in Jesus' name.

Thank God for your life, learn to live a holy life and always be prayerful.

Sing: *My life time, I will give God my life time...*

For Victory and Abundant Blessings in all life's situations

Chapter 49

BLESSING ON A NEWLY BUILT, BOUGHT, LEASED HOUSE OR LAND

Read: Ps. 127, Haggai 2:9
Sing: All I have they are given to me by Lord...

It is a good thing to a have something like land or house newly purchased or built respectively. It is the sign of favour on our lives. But many people today had entered into curses, evil covenants and battle of life by living in a demon control house or environment. A lot people had purchased death with their own money. But you don't have to fear if you will hand over everything to God. Give your own life to Him now to save you from the torments of the enemy. The only thing that the enemy fears is the name of Jesus.

Sing: * All I have they are given to me by Lord...

PRAY THESE PRAYERS:
1. Lord, all good gifts come from you, I thank you for this new gift of (...)* in Jesus' name
2. Call the name of Jesus three times and say: All powers and principalities that have been working in this environment, I bind you and destroy your powers, in Jesus' name.
3. Call the blood of Jesus three times and say: I soak this house/land in the blood of Jesus and I declare it free from the hand of the devil from now on, in Jesus' name.
4. O earth! *(Three times)*, hear ye the word of God as I stand upon you today. You have taken the blood of Jesus, I am a child of God, because of the blood of covenant, I destroy everything you may want to harbour against me and my home, in Jesus' name.
5. I plead the blood of Jesus on the foundation of this house/land, and

For Victory and Abundant Blessings in all life's situations

I destroy by the blood of Jesus, all evil, seen and unseen present on it, in Jesus' name.

6. I receive the power to increase in all things, as I move into you; I shall not be reduced or decreased, in Jesus' name.
7. I command the peace and comfort of God upon this house/land, in Jesus' name.
8. I entered this house/land with joy I shall not be forced out of it in sorrow and frustration, in Jesus' name
9. Every power that works evil that wants to follow me from where I am coming from to this new place, I command you to turn back forever, in Jesus' name.
10. I receive this house/land as my Goshen and Cannon land, in Jesus' name.
11. Let the water, air, the sun and other elements in this environment, work for my comfort, progress and peace, in Jesus' name.
12. Lord, let your eyes of love, protect and bless this place, in Jesus' name.
13. I surround this environment with Holy Ghost fire, in Jesus' name

Thank God for answering your prayers.

Sing: * What a mighty God we serve...

Chapter **50**

BLESSING FOR NEWLY MARRIED COUPLE

Read: Gen. 1:18-25. Gen. 31:48, Ps. 90:9, Ps. 127:1, Ps. 98:3, Ps. 4:6-7, Ruth 4:11-12

Sing: * It is well, it is well...
* We are saying thank you Jesus...

Marriage is an institution ordained by God. So it is a good thing to be married. The Bible says, if a man finds a good wife, it is a favour from God. Also, a faithful husband is a gift from God. But a lot of marriages today, died prematurely, just because the devil attacks them and since they were not found or not well found on Jesus Christ, the storm of life scattered them. Why not found your marriage on the Rock of life today? That is, Jesus Christ and on His word, as you are starting a new life.

*Sing: *All I have they are given to me by my Lord...*

PRAY THESE PRAYERS:
1. Thank the Lord for making you to see the day of your joy.
2. Thank Him for putting to shame all the powers of *"No"* that has been saying it will not come to pass.
3. Arise O God! the great builder of glorious homes, place the foundation block of the life of this marriage in the foundation of your Son Jesus Christ, in Jesus' name.
4. This marriage shall not die a premature death, in Jesus' name.
5. Every arrow of premature death fashioned against this home, shall not prosper, in Jesus' name.
6. Today, we command new and glorious things to begin to happen in this new home, in Jesus' name.

■ For Victory and Abundant Blessings in all life s situations   New Breakthrough Prayers

7. We have been joined together today; we destroy every evil power that will want to separate us in the future, in Jesus' name.
8. O Lord! let our first love and joy never fade, in Jesus' name.
9. Let the presence of the Lord accompany us in this journey and let us not be put to shame, in Jesus' name.
10. Let the spirit of wisdom, knowledge and understanding to live a peaceful, joyful and comfortable life come upon us, in Jesus' name.
11. We receive the power to be fruitful, physically and spiritually, in Jesus' name.
12. We reject the incoming of strange woman, man, children, friend or relation into this home, in Jesus' name.
13. Call the name of Jesus three times and say: Lord, let the blood of Jesus cover this home now and forever, in Jesus' name.
14. O Lord! bind us together with a cord of love that can never be broken, in Jesus' name.
15. We bind and banish every spirit of immorality and unfaithfulness from this home, in Jesus' name.
16. Let the spirits of submission, respect and humility for each other fall upon us in this home, in Jesus' name.
17. Let no divination or enchantment directed against this home prosper, in Jesus' name.
18. You spirits of divorce, misunderstanding, anger and separation, we reject you all from this home, in Jesus' name.
19. O Lord! let every good thing that used to accompany the marriage of the children of God fall upon this marriage, in Jesus' name.

Begin to thank God for a happy marital life and praise Him with songs of praise.

Sing: * This is my day of Joy...

For Victory and Abundant Blessings in all life's situations

Chapter 51

BLESSING FOR A NEWLY BORN BABY

Read: Mk. 10:14, Ps. 22:6, Prov. 29:15, Luke. 1:42, Ps. 127:3, Gen. 22:18, Isaiah 49:23, 54:13

Sing: * All I have they are given to me by my Lord...
* We are saying thank you Jesus...

Children are gifts from God. They are meant to bless us and our generation. They carry a message from God. A destiny meant to better their family and generation. But as much as they are blessings, they could become a curse if care is not taken. The birth of a child and the nurturing of them must be spiritually handled and committed unto God. There is a contention for their lives and destinies and we must not allow the devil to take them away from us.

Sing: * All I have they are given to me by my Lord...

PRAY THESE PRAYERS:

1. O Lord! I thank you for this gift of a baby, it is your doing and it is marvellous in our sight, your name is praised, in Jesus' name.
2. Lord, I thank you for the conception and the delivery of this child, thank you, in Jesus' name.
3. When Jesus was born the three wise men came to give Him special gifts, let heaven arise today to give this baby three special gift of divine wisdom, knowledge and understanding, in Jesus' name.
4. Call the blood of Jesus three times and say: Let the blood of Jesus cleanse this baby from all generational curses and evil covenants contacted through blood and at delivery, in Jesus' name.
5. Nobody can cover the glory of the sun and that of the moon, Lord, do not allow the enemy to cover the glory of this child.

For Victory and Abundant Blessings in all life's situations

6. Lord, this baby has brought joy to everybody today, it will not become a sorrow and disgrace to its parent and generation, in Jesus' name.

7. I rebuke every power that has gone ahead of time to cause evil in the life of this child, in Jesus' name.

8. Lord, the Bible says that the child Jesus had favour from the Lord and from man, let this child receives favour from God and from man, in Jesus' name.

9. This child came in a pool of blood; let him not go back in a pool of blood, in Jesus' name.

10. Lord, make this child like a bow in the hand of a mighty man, in Jesus' name.

11. Father, let every curse of disobedience to God and to parent in the future of this child be destroyed by the blood of Jesus, in Jesus' name.

12. Child, receive the blessing of divine fruitfulness in life, in Jesus' name.

13. O Lord! let the heaven rise to direct the course of this child in life, in Jesus' name.

14. Every power of the enemy that may want to avenge the past misdeed of this child's parent or generation from him, you are all render powerless and your plan destroy as from today on, in Jesus' name.

15. O Lord! do not let this child live a life of vanity, let him (or her) know and lives for your glory, in Jesus name

Begin to commit the life journey of the child into the hands of the Lord and thank Him because he has heard.

|115|

Chapter 52

PRAYERS FOR THOSE CELEBRATING THEIR BIRTHDAY

Read: Ps. 90:12, Eccl. 12:1, Job 5:18-27
Sing **I am saying thank you Jesus...*
* This is the day (twice) that the Lord has made...
* Oh Lord I am very very grateful...

Many don't really count the day they were born as important. So, they don't see reason in giving thanks to God. Your coming to this world matters a lot, not to you alone, but to your generation because of what the Lord has planned to use you for. The devil is using the day of birth of many people, to fight them and their destiny. So, learn to thank God for your coming to the world and the life He has given you. But if you have not given that life back to Him, do it today.

Sing: **I am saying thank you Jesus...*
* This is the day that the Lord has made...

PRAY THESE PRAYERS:
1. Lord, I thank you for my coming to the world and the life given to me, in Jesus' name.
2. O Lord, I thank you for your protection over my life from the day I was conceived to the day I was born and up till today, in Jesus' name.
3. Lord, I thank you for all you have done for me and all that you will still do.
4. Call the blood of Jesus *(seven times)* and say: I cover my now, and future, the work of my hand and destiny with the blood of Jesus, in Jesus' name.
5. Lord, I receive the spirit of wisdom, knowledge and understanding to live my life according to your purpose, in Jesus' name.
6. I shall not be cut-off in the middle of my years; I shall come back to you in ripe age, in Jesus' name.

For Victory and Abundant Blessings in all life's situations

7. I shall fulfil my destiny to its fullness, in Jesus' name.
8. Every spirit, power or principality troubling my coming to this world I bind you and destroy your power and plan, in Jesus' name.
9. Every plan of the enemy station at the bus-stop of my future endeavours, I cancel you with the blood of Jesus, in the name of Jesus.
10. O Lord! Let heaven rise to see me to the fulfilment of my destiny, in Jesus' name.
11. I receive the power, wisdom and knowledge to live a prosperous life, in Jesus' name.
12. I shall not become victim of evil circumstances and situations of life, in Jesus' name.
13. Father Lord, let your goodness and mercy follow me all the days of my life, in Jesus' name.
14. Every sin or evil that came with my coming to the world and that wants to mortgage my future and destiny, I stand against you and destroy your plan by the blood of Jesus, in Jesus' name.
15. Everything that needs your touch in my life, Lord, touch them, in Jesus' name.
16. I cry on my way to the world, Lord, do not let me cry on my way back to you, in Jesus' name.
17. All the spirits different from the Spirit of God that want to follow me on the journey of my life, in order to destroy my Godly destiny I bind and destroy your plan, in Jesus' name.
18. I receive peace, joy and abundant blessing for the rest of my journey in life, in Jesus' name.
19. Holy Spirit, I renew your presence and company upon my life as I continue with my life journey, in Jesus' name.
20. Today, let my name be inscribed in the Book of Life by the blood of Jesus.
21. O Lord! help me not to live a life of vanity and not to regret coming into this world, in Jesus' name.

Begin to thank God for what he has done.

Sing: *Because He lives I can face tomorrow...*

For Victory and Abundant Blessings in all life's situations

Chapter 53

DELIVERANCE PRAYERS FOR HANDS

Read: Job 37:7. Psalm 144.1
Sing: * Holy Ghost and Fire, fill body, fill my soul, fill my life.

Hands symbolize power, skill, action, purpose, blessing, expression etc. When you clasp your hands, it symbolized unity and allegiance. When you clench your hands, it symbolizes tension or suppression. When you raise your hands above your head, it symbolizes surrender. When you raise your hands to the side, it symbolizes inclusion and acceptance. When you put your hands on the chest, it symbolizes destiny and sincerity. When you fold your hands, it symbolizes contemplation or you being passive and not knowing what next to do. So, if something goes wrong with your hands spiritually, the manifestation physically will be terrible and serious..

Some people are actually handcuffed in the spirit realm. For such people, nothing is going to work physically because their hands are already tied up.

PRAY THESE PRAYERS:
1. You grave holding my hands and its fruitfulness captive, open up and vomit them to me by fire!
2. You my dead and decayed hands, resurrect and become perfectly healed in the name of Jesus!
3. You my hands that have been rendered dead and fruitless, resurrect and be fruitful in the name of Jesus!
4. You scorpions assigned against my hands, release me and die by fire!

For Victory and Abundant Blessings in all life s situations

5. You evil arrows fashioned against my hands, I command you to go back to your senders in the name of Jesus!
6. You spiritual worms assigned to devour my hands, come out and die!
7. You spiritual devourers assigned to devour my hands and render it fruitless, come out and die!
8. You evil object buried against the fruitfulness of my hands, be up-rooted and scatter by fire!
9. You evil personalities hiding in my hands, come out and die!
10. You evil trenches housing enemy ambush against my hands, bury my enemies alive in Jesus´ name
11. Evil contractors hired against my hands, I terminate your contracts from source by fire! Die in the name of Jesus!
12. You spirit of hindrance hindering the fruitfulness of my hands, release it and die!
13. You spirit of hindrance hindering my breakthrough, release it and die!
14. You spirit of hindrance holding on to my birthright, release it and die!
15. Outside witchcraft powers co-operating with household witchcraft against my hands, scatter and die!
16. Household witchcraft gathering against my hands, scatter and die!
17. Household witchcraft verdict and conclusion against my hands, be nullified by fire!
18. Witchcraft covens linked to the death and fruitlessness of my hands, catch fire and scatter!
19. You evil objects being used to monitor my hands for evil, be scattered and rendered invalid!
20. You evil priests ministering against my hands from any evil altar, fall down and die!
21. You evil altars erected against the fruitfulness of my hands be up-rooted and scatter!
22. I pursue, I overtake and I recover by fire whatever the enemy has stolen from my hands in the name of Jesus!
23. My hands, defy any spiritual call to death or unfruitfulness in the name of Jesus!

24. My hands, refuse to co-operate with my enemies against me in the name of Jesus!
25. My hands, you would always bring me blessings and not problems and curses in the name of Jesus!
26. My original HANDS, wherever you are, escape witchcraft captivity and locate me now by fire, in the name of Jesus!

Continue to wash your hands with the blood of Jesus when you go out and come in everyday. Thank God for the deliverance and victory. Sing powerful victory songs to the shame of the devil.

■ For Victory and Abundant Blessings in all life s situations

Chapter 54

DELIVERANCE PRAYERS FOR LEGS OR FEET UNDER ATTACK

Read: Psalm 24, Romans 10:15, Joshua 1:3
Song: I have a God who never fails

Legs or feet are symbol of dominion, authority, ruler ship, can be spiritually and demonically caged, it can be tied, defiled, it can be amputated, paralysed, weakened, chained, it can be injured, it can be cobweb, it can be broken or twisted, it can be suspended, it can be covenanted for evil, it can be remotely controlled, it can be exchanged, it can also poisoned and then **IT CAN BE UNDER CURSE.**

If the legs or feet are not beautiful, It will always walk into trouble and danger. Any environment they walk to, there will be death and bad luck. When they walked into business it collapse. When they walked into marriage it collapse. *Deut 28:19*. It can walk into danger, it also bring danger and confusion..Another thing is that they will be arriving late at the place of honour

They walk into frustration and disappointment. When they do business, the business is not stable. They just go all about from one place to another. Their entrance brings sorrow, their exit brings joy. They bring bad luck, failure, bankruptcy.

They bring accident in both private and commercial or any vehicle they entered.

PRAY THESE PRAYERS:
1. Chains from the grave operating on my legs, break away now in the name of Jesus. *(3ce)*.
2. Serpent and scorpions assigned against my legs die now in Jesus mighty name. *(3ce)*.

3. Any masquerading power covering my legs come out disappear in Jesus name. *(3ce)*
4. I fire back every evil arrow of witchcraft fire into my legs in Jesus name. *(3ce)*
5. Every curse upon my legs, break in Jesus name. *(7ce)*
6. My legs begin to divide my Jordan of life in Jesus name. *(7ce)*.
7. My legs *(7ce)* hear the word of the Lord work into your breakthrough in Jesus name. *(7ce)*

Cover your legs with the blood of Jesus several times and Praise the name of the Lord for true victories.

For Victory and Abundant Blessings in all life's situations

Chapter 55

DELIVERANCE PRAYERS FOR HEADS UNDER ATTACK

Read: Psalm 92:10
Sing: * I plead the blood of Jesus...
* Oh! the blood of Jesus...

Head is very important part of the body. It is a symbol destiny and glory. it contains the face which distinguish each person, through head you can know people. It contains the brain the power of the body.

It is the most important both physically m and spiritually. The head houses the brain, the eyes for sight, houses the ears for hearing, houses the nose for smelling and the mouth for speaking and eating.

PRAY THESE PRAYERS:

1. Evil hands anointed to waste my head, wither, in the name of Jesus.
2. Every arrow of untimely death, fired at my head, backfire, in the name of Jesus.
3. My head, my head, my head, hear the Word of the Lord, arise and shine, in the name of Jesus.
4. Any dark invisible covering, on my head, catch fire, in the name of Jesus.
5. Every curse, operating against my head, die, by the power in the blood of Jesus, in the name of Jesus.
6. Every manipulation of my glory through my hair, scatter now, in the name of Jesus.
7. Every hand of the strongman upon my head, dry up, in the name of Jesus.
8. Every power of death, assigned against my head, die, in the name of Jesus.
9. Chains upon my head, break, in the name of Jesus.

10. Holy Ghost fire, arise, kill every satanic deposit in my head, in the name of Jesus.
11. My head, receive deliverance by fire, in the name of Jesus.
12. Every power, summoning my head, from the gate of the grave, die, in the name of Jesus.
13. Thou power of God, arise, attack all covens assigned against my head, in the name of Jesus.
14. Every ordinance, invoked by the power of darkness into the heavens against my head, I wipe you off, in the name of Jesus.
15. Rain of wisdom, knowledge, and favour, fall upon my head, in the name of Jesus.
16. Voices of strangers, casting spells against my head, die, in the name of Jesus.
17. Blood of Jesus, Water of life, fire of God, wash my head, in the name of Jesus.
18. I shake off, bullets of darkness from my head, in the name of Jesus.
19. Every power, using my hair against me, die, in the name of Jesus.
20. Invisible loads of darkness, upon my head, catch fire, in the name of Jesus.
21. My head, my head, receive the touch of the resurrection power of the Lord Jesus Christ, in the name of Jesus.
22. Every arrow, fired into my head, go back to the sender, in the name of Jesus.
23. I decree, that insanity is not my lot, so every arrow of insanity, go back to the sender, in the name of Jesus.
24. My head, be lifted up above my enemies around me, in the name of Jesus.
25. My head be lifted up, above the unbelievers around me, in the name of Jesus.
26. My head, hear the Word of the Lord, arise, possess your possession, and possess your destiny, in the name of Jesus.
27. Every handwriting of darkness, working against my head, backfire, in the name of Jesus.

28. I plug my head, into the resurrection power of the Lord Jesus Christ, in the name of Jesus.

Plead the blood of Jesus over your head by placing your hands on your head pleading the blood of Jesus for three minutes. Call fire of the Holy Spirit for 2 minutes.

Praise the name of the Lord for the victories.

For Victory and Abundant Blessings in all life's situations

Chapter 56

DELIVERANCE PRAYERS FOR LANDS UNDER DEMONIC ATTACK

Read: Lev.18:27, Psalm 24
Sing: * The wall of Jericho fell down flat...
* I've been to Calvary...
* God of Elijah send down fire
* I plead the blood of Jesus

Lands can be deviled, cursed, scorpioned,, Serpented, possessed of evils, tormenting miscarriage, demoting, polluting, bewitching, wicked. It is very important to know mystery about lands. Not all lands good for building, farming or doing any projects until it is well delivered by the power in the name and blood of Jesus Christ.

PRAY THESE PRAYERS:
1. All virtues, that are buried under the earth, in my environment, I exhume you, by power and fire, in the name of Jesus.
2. Thou power, of environmental graveyards, die, in the name of Jesus.
3. Every environmental agenda, forcing princes to trek while servants are on the horses, be overturned, in the name of Jesus.
4. Holy Ghost fire, sanitize my environment by the power in the blood of Jesus.
5. Every satanic dedication of this land lands, by ancestors, to the devil, I break that dedication, in the name of Jesus.
6. I remove, every cover of darkness upon the land, in the name of Jesus.
7. Thou land of my habitation, I set you free from every idol pollution, the name of Jesus.

8. Every altar, built on the land, which has brought a cover of darkness, scatter, in the name of Jesus.
9. Every power, which has worked over the land of my habitation in the dark world, I recover you, and be redeemed by the blood of Jesus.
10. Every band of wickedness, over my environment, break, in Jesus name.
11. My neck, shall not be broken by territorial spirits, in the name of Jesus.
12. Blood, poured on the ground will not eat me up, in the name of Jesus.
13. Every charm buried in the ground to subdue my life, I destroy you, in the name of Jesus.
14. I quench, every anger energised through the land, against me, in Jesus name.
15. Every landlord spirit, troubling my health, be paralysed, in the name of Jesus.
16. Every government of darkness, upon the land of my habitation, be dismantled, in the name of Jesus.
- Lord, let the sanctifying power, of the blood of Jesus, move upon my environment, in the name of Jesus.
- Lord, let the purifying power, of the blood of Jesus, take control of my environment, in the name of Jesus.
17. Every evil spiritual occupant, of the land where I dwell, I bind you and cast you into the desert, in the name of Jesus.
18. Every activity of witchcraft, upon my environment, I paralyse you and I disgrace you, in the name of Jesus.
19. Every strange visitation, upon the land of my habitation, I paralyse your power, in the name of Jesus.
20. Every evil consultation, of power of darkness, taking place in my environment, I silence you, in the name of Jesus.
21. Father, I agree with the Word of the Lord, that every power causing strange activities in my environment, will be quenched, in the name of Jesus.

22. Every gate, of water spirits and cultic powers upon the land, be closed, in the name of Jesus.
23. All the high places of water spirits upon the land, I bind you and pull you down, in the name of Jesus.
24. Every familiar spirit, operating in the land, I pull down your power, in the name of Jesus.
25. Every power, releasing sickness in my environment, carry your sickness and disappear, in the name of Jesus.
26. Every satanic whirlwind, stirred up in my environment, I bind your power, in the name of Jesus.
27. Every spiritual gate, upon this land, I pull you down, in the name of Jesus.
28. Every curse of neglect, upon this land, break, in the name of Jesus.
29. Every curse of suffering, upon the land of my habitation, break, in the name of Jesus.
30. Every curse of babel, which is division, upon the land of my habitation, break, in the name of Jesus.
31. Every curse of waywardness upon the land of my habitation, break, in the name of Jesus.
32. Every curse of marital problem, upon the land of my habitation, break, in the name of Jesus.
33. Every curse of hardship, upon the land of my habitation, break, in the name of Jesus.
34. Every curse of spiritual and physical barrenness, upon the land of my habitation, break, in the name of Jesus.
35. Every curse and covenant of sickness, upon the land of my habitation, break, in the name of Jesus.
36. Every curse and covenant of strange happenings, upon the land of my habitation, break, in the name of Jesus.
37. Every curse of wickedness, upon the land of my habitation, break, in the name of Jesus.
38. Every curse of tragedy, upon the land of my habitation, break, in the name of Jesus.

* For Victory and Abundant Blessings in all life's situations

39. Every curse of hindrances, upon the land of my habitation, break, in the name of Jesus.
40. Every curse of backwardness, upon the land of my habitation, break, in the name of Jesus.
41. Every curse of failure, upon the land of my habitation, break, in the name of Jesus.
42. Every curse of failure, at the edge of breakthrough, upon the land of my habitation, break, in the name of Jesus.
43. I overthrow, I bind, I destroy, the influence of occult powers upon this land, in the name of Jesus.
44. Father, let Your fire, deal with the witches and wizards upon this land, in the name of Jesus.
45. Every throne and caldron of darkness, upon the land, catch fire, in the name of Jesus.
46. Father, I stand as Your child, and I destroy the ability of the wicked upon this land, in the name of Jesus.
47. Every satanic veil, upon this land, catch fire, in the name of Jesus. Praise the name of the Lord plead the blood of Jesus and ask Holy Ghost fire to take absolute control of the land.

Don't forget to be praying always while you walk on the land. Continue to confess that you claim your land back

Thank God for the victory

Chapter 57

DELIVERANCE PRAYERS FROM DEMONIC ATTACK OF SPIRITUAL COBWEB

Read: (Psalm 109:1-31)
Sing: * Holy Ghost arise in your power 2ce.
Power to deliver, power to save
Power to deliver, power to set me free
Holy Ghost arise in your power
Let the Spirit of the Lord come down

Cobweb is a common thing around us but could be an instrument of the enemies many times. Many times at home, outside, as you walk along you just fall into cobwebs, or you find it at doors, windows, over buckets of waters or your business. Cobwebs are very strong instrument of the enemies unknowingly to many. It is demonic spiritual Network. Don't take any chance with the enemies again. Spiders must not be allowed in your vicinity. Be careful pray. Victory is sure in the mighty name of Jesus Christ.

PRAY THESE PRAYERS:
1. Let every demonic cobweb assigned against my life be wasted by unquenchable fire in Jesus name.
2. Every attacker of my goodness through cobweb fall down and die in Jesus name.
3. Let every patrolling web assigned against my life and business be paralysed in Jesus name.
4. Every suspended power using cobweb against my life collide with the rock of ages and fall down and die in Jesus name.
5. Every foundational power manipulating my life with cobweb be destroyed by fire in the name of Jesus.

6. Any demonic and marine cobwebs floating along my passage be burnt by fire in Jesus name.
7. Let every destributor of evil cobweb within and inside my house fall down and die in Jesus name.
8. Anything deposited in my body through cobwebs be destroyed by fire in Jesus name.
9. Every witchcraft and marine cobweb assigned to divert me from my part of breakthrough be consumed by fire in Jesus name.
10. Every bewitched cobweb assigned to hinder my progress be roasted by fire in Jesus name.

You will have a financial breakthrough this year in Jesus mighty name.

For Victory and Abundant Blessings in all life's situations

Chapter 58

DELIVERANCE PRAYERS FROM POVERTY

Read: GEN. 26:1, 12; PRO. 11:24; HAGGAI 1:6; 2KGS. 4; 1 KGS. 7; LK. 5; GEN. 8:22

Sing: * Glory be to God in the highest Amen.....
* That wonderful name Jesus

PRAY THESE PRAYERS:
1. Every unconscious marriage with poverty, die in Jesus name.
2. My Father, make me enter into sweat less prosperity in Jesus name.
3. My Father, use me to good things that nobody has never done in my family before in Jesus name.
4. My Pharaoh of profitless hard work, fall and rise no more in Jesus name.
5. Every virtue of my life buried by household wickedness, come out now in Jesus name.
6. Every wealth stolen from me since I was a baby, I repossess it back to me now in Jesus name.
7. O Heavens over my prosperity, open now by fire in Jesus name.
8. O wealth, jump out of the habitation of the wicked and locate me now in Jesus name.
9. You children of darkness, continue to labour and at the end of the labour, transfer the wealth to me in Jesus name.
10. I dig the sweat of my enemy by the power in the name of Jesus.
11. Angels of the Living God, pursue wealth into my hands in Jesus name.
12. Any power that wants me to die as a pauper, you are a liar, die in Jesus name.
13. No matter my background, no matter my family, no matter my education.

14. O God arise and lift me up in Jesus name.
15. I rise out of the dust of poverty by the power in the blood of Jesus, in Jesus name.

Thank you for praying. Something great is about to happen to you, that's my believe.

Welcome to your season of Victories on every side in Jesus name.

Chapter 59

DELIVERANCE PRAYERS FOR THE FIRSTBORN

Read: *Colossians. 2:14-15, Galatians. 3:13-14*
Song: ** Arise O Lord and my enemies be scatter*
* We lift up your name higher

Firstborns occupy very significant position in God's agenda. They are born to lead and rule; they are called to serve God and be his inheritance. They are sent to pioneer and champion godly courses that will bring godly changes among human beings.

PRAY THESE PRAYERS:
1. Lord, you are the covenant remover, every way in which family and generational curses are working evil in my life and job, Lord block the ways by your blood, remove all curses in my life in Jesus' name.
2. I take myself out today from covenants troubling my life for a long time in Jesus' name.
3. Spirit behind known and unknown covenants operating in my life, I command you, get out of my life now in Jesus' name
4. Every padlock of the enemy that has put my family and me in the bondage of curse be opened right now in Jesus' name.
5. All covenants that my family may have entered into with herbalists or spiritualists that are bringing curses upon me, I destroy them with the blood of Jesus' today.
6. All generational, self-imposed covenants working evil in my life, be terminated now in Jesus' name.
7. Every association with evil covenants troubling my life be destroyed in Jesus' name.
8. Plead the blood of Jesus Christ.

■ For Victory and Abundant Blessings in all life's situations

9. Lord, turn every channel of sorrow in my life to joy in the name of Jesus
10. 2. Lord, let the later part of my life be better than the beginning in Jesus name.
11. 3. From all the oppressors of mankind that deny me my covenant rights and benefits, cause them to restore seven fold in Jesus name.
12. 4. Every battle I have pleaded with or persuaded and have refused to go, God destroy it in Jesus name.
13. 5. All battles that gather around and cooperate against the affairs of my life, storm of heaven, sweep them away in Jesus name.
14. 6. It is joy and gladness that always, attend the birth of a new baby, my Lord, from today by the reason of your favour, make me become a man of honour and praise everywhere in Jesus name.
15. 7. At every place where I have been rejected and forsaken,
16. Lord by the reason of your favour let me become a star in Jesus name.
17. I break myself loose from every curse and unprofitable covenant in
18. Jesus' name.
19. Let the blood of Jesus wash my name from satanic records.
20. Let every curse attached to my place and time of birth, be broken in Jesus' name.
21. I break with the blood of Jesus every curse of impossibility in my life and that of my family.
22. I break with the blood of Jesus every curse of failure in my life and that of my family. (7 times)
23. I break with the blood of Jesus every curse of infirmity, sickness and
24. diseases in my life, and that of my family.
25. I break with the blood of Jesus every curse of giving up at the edge of break through, in Jesus name (3 times) ˙
26. I break with the blood of Jesus , every curse of financial failure in our family in Jesus name (3 times)
27. I break with the blood of Jesus every curse of poverty and bankruptcy in our business in Jesus name. (3 times)
28. I break with the blood of Jesus every curse of error upon my life in

Jesus name. (3 times)

29. I break with the blood of Jesus every curse of untimely death in our family in Jesus name. (3 times)
30. I break with the blood of Jesus multiple curses upon my life in Jesus name. *(7 times)*
31. I break with the blood of Jesus every iron like curse upon my life in Jesus name.

Begin to worship the King of kings and Lord of all. Your victory is sure. You will recover, you will be positioned you shall be honoured.

Chapter **60**

DELIVERING YOUR POSITIVE DESTINY THROUGH ONE HUNDRED PRAYER QUAKES

Read: John17, Isaiah 60:1-2
"Arise, shine; for thy light is come, and the glory of the Lord is upon thee. For behold, the darkness shall cover the earth and gross darkness the people: but the Lord shall rise upon thee, and His glory shall be seen upon thee".

Sing: ** There is something that makes me come to your presence..*
       * Because He lives I can face tomorrow

PRAY THESE PRAYERS:

1. I recover my destiny, from the destiny robbers and manipulators, in the name of Jesus.
2. My life, become too hot for the enemy to handle, in the name of Jesus.
3. Every horn, pressing down the glory of my life, scatter, in the name of Jesus.
4. Lord, let the blood of Jesus, cleanse my life from the evil effects of past immoral life, in the name of Jesus.
5. I renounce, every anti-breakthrough habit in my life, in the name of Jesus.
6. Heavenly Surgeons, do every necessary surgical operation in my life, for my breakthrough to manifest, in the name of Jesus.
7. Wherever, my glory is tied, thunder fire of God, lose them now, in the name of Jesus.
8. Where the Lord God of Elijah is, arise and enlarge my coast by fire, in the name of Jesus
9. Every spirit of detained and delayed blessings, I cast you out of my life, in the name of Jesus.

| 137 |

10. Every hidden ancestral and blood covenants, hindering my prosperity, break, in the name of Jesus.
11. Every demonic monitoring gadget, assigned against my prosperity, scatter, in the name of Jesus.
12. Every evil monitoring, monitoring my prosperity for destruction, catch fire, in the name of Jesus.
13. Arise O God, and let the enemies of my prosperity, scatter, in the name of Jesus.
14. Every yoke of poverty, break by the blood of Jesus, in the name of Jesus.
15. My destiny, hear the Word of the Lord, your time of weeping has expired, bring forth glory by fire, in the name of Jesus.
16. Every marine spirit, assigned against my prosperity scatter, in Jesus name.
17. Every night caterer, assigned against my prosperity, scatter, in Jesus name.
18. Every eaters of flesh and drinker of blood, feeding on my prosperity, die, in the name of Jesus.
19. Every strongman, hindering my prosperity, fall down and die, in Jesus name.
20. Every evil power, projecting into my dreams, fall down and die, in Jesus name.
21. Any material, from my body, being against my prosperity, catch fire, in the name of Jesus.
22. I nullify, premature and stillbirth breakthrough, in the name of Jesus.
23. I release my destiny, from any evil chain, in the name of Jesus.
24. I release my destiny, from any evil padlock, in the name of Jesus.
25. I release my destiny, from any witchcraft cage, in the name of Jesus.
26. My destiny, hear the Word of the Lord, arise and shine, in the name of Jesus.
27. Thou power of failure, at the edge of breakthrough in my life, break, in Jesus name.
28. Spirits of failure, at the edge of breakthrough, lose your hold upon my life, in the name of Jesus.
29. Every satanic poison, in my body, be neutralised, by the blood of Jesus.

■ For Victory and Abundant Blessings in all life's situations

30. My spirit man, receive strength to bring forth glory, in the name of Jesus.
31. I fireback, every arrow of death, in the name of Jesus.
32. Every blood covenant, speaking against my destiny, break, in Jesus name.
33. Lord, if my life is not functioning, correct with the blood of Jesus.
34. I withdraw, every power, which is in charge of poverty in my life, in Jesus name.
35. Every spirit of failure, in my life, be destroyed in the name of Jesus.
36. Every spirit of barrenness of good things in my life, be destroyed and replaced with the spirit of abundant goodness, in Jesus name.
37. Every spirit of poverty, be destroyed and be replaced with the spirit of prosperity, in Jesus name.
38. Every power, that has desired to put me into shame, be destroyed, by the blood of Jesus.
39. I destroy, any power that is in charge of destroying good things, in the name of Jesus.
40. Any power, siphoning my blessings, lose your hold, in the name of Jesus.
41. Blood of Jesus.
42. Blood of Jesus, arise in Your bulldozing power, sanitize my destiny, in the name of Jesus.
43. Holy Ghost fire, sanitise my life for supernatural prosperity, in Jesus name.
44. Lord, by the power that answered Jabez, visit my life by fire, in Jesus name.
45. Creative power of God, repair any damage done to my life and
46. destiny structures, in the name of Jesus.
47. God, arise and advertise Your creative power in my life, in the name of Jesus.
48. I pull down, the strongholds of barrenness of good things, in the name of Jesus.
49. Every witchcraft power, bewitching my life, fall down and die, in the name of Jesus.
50. Lord, by Your which knows no impossibility, let my glory manifest, in the name of Jesus.

| 139 |

For Victory and Abundant Blessings in all life's situations

51. This month, shall not pass by; I must bring forth glory, in the name of Jesus.
52. My Father, bring forth signs and wonder in my life, in the name of Jesus.
53. I invite the power of God, into every department of my life, in Jesus name.
54. Healing power of God, flow into my spirit man, in the name of Jesus.
55. I call forth my glory, from any captivity, in the name of Jesus.
56. Every clinical prophecy, covering my situation, be overturned by fire, in Jesus name.
57. Where is the Lord God of Elijah? Give me the miracle of supernatural prosperity, in Jesus name.
58. My Father, speak life and productiveness into my life, in the name of Jesus.
59. Every evil hand, laid upon my destiny, catch fire, in Jesus name.
60. God of deliverance, deliver me from every generational liability, in the name of Jesus.
61. I release my life, from the grip of evil plantations, in the name of Jesus.
62. I reject, every arrow assigned to torment my life, in the name of Jesus.
63. My head, life, destiny, and blood, receive the fire of deliverance, in Jesus name.
64. Every tree, which the enemy has planted against my prosperity, be uprooted, in Jesus name.
65. Every witchcraft decision, on my prosperity, be cancelled, by fire, in the name of Jesus.
66. God of prosperity, bring honey out of Rock for me, in the name of Jesus.
67. Any problem, which came into my life through past feeding on the table of the devil, receive solution, in the name of Jesus.
68. Any problem, that came into my life through ungodliness, receive solution, in the name of Jesus.
69. Any problem, that came into my life, through deposits of spirit wife or husband, be resolved, by fire, in the name of Jesus.
70. Any problem, that came into my life, through evil spiritual surgery, be resolved, in Jesus name.

- For Victory and Abundant Blessings in all life's situations

71. Every power, assigned, to embarrass me maritaly, I kill you now, in the name of Jesus.
72. My Father, let me experience the glory power of Jehovah, in the name of Jesus.
73. Holy Ghost fire, incubate my head, life and destiny, for productivity, in the name of Jesus.
74. Any power, stealing from my body, catch fire, in the name of Jesus..
75. Every glory, which has departed from my life, return by fire, in the name of Jesus.
76. My Father, arise and advertise Your power, in my life, in the name of Jesus.
77. I arise by fire and possess my possessions of prosperity, in the name of Jesus.
78. My Father, bombard me, with anointing of prosperity, in the name of Jesus.
79. Holy Ghost fire, arise, burn away every anti-prosperity infirmity, in the name of Jesus.
80. I speak destruction, unto any mountain of disappointment in my life, in the name of Jesus.
81. I speak death, unto any mountain of disgrace in my life, in the name of Jesus.
82. I speak paralysis, unto every mountain of embarrassment, in Jesus name.
83. I decree civil war, against every company of the wicked, working against my life, in Jesus name.
84. O God, arise and release the earthquake of deliverance to deliver me, in the name of Jesus name.
85. God's light will shine on my path and His favour will encompass me all the days of my life, in the name of Jesus.
86. Foreigners, shall build up walls for me and their Kings shall minister unto me, in the name of Jesus.
87. God shall set me upon a Rock and shall lift up my head above my enemies all around me. He shall tread down my enemies, and render their camp desolate, in the name of Jesus

88. God's thoughts for me is of peace and not of evil, to give my expected end, in the name of Jesus.
89. Henceforth I refuse to live in fear. Rather my fear shall be upon my enemies, in the name of Jesus.
90. God wishes above all things that I may prospered mine in the name of Jesus. I receive prosperity in the name of Jesus.
91. God has not given me the spirit of bondage, to fear. The word of God is quick and powerful in my mouth. God has put the power of His word in my mouth, in the name of Jesus.
92. My appearance is as appearance of a Horse. So I leap, I run like mighty men. When I fall upon the sword, it can not hurt me in the name of Jesus.
93. I cannot be threatened, my persecutors shall all stumble, fumble and fall. Their everlasting confusion and disgrace shall never be forgotten. God has commanded me to fear not, for He is in total control of my life in the name of Jesus.
94. No counsel of the wicked shall stand against me, in the name of Jesus.
95. God has equipped me, and made me a danger and a terror to all my enemies in the name of Jesus.
96. I totally trust in the Lord and I am not leaning on my own understanding . I fill my heart with words of faith; I receive and speak the words of faith in the name of Jesus.
97. The young Lions do lack and suffer hunger, but I who seek after the Lord Almighty, shall not lack any good thing, in the name of Jesus.
98. God is my Rock and my house of defence from now on till the end of my life., in the name of Jesus.
99. Say powerfully JESUS 21 times, HOLY GHOST FIRE 21times and HALLELUYAH!!!! *21 times.*
100. Begin to give God quality Praises an Worship, for the nest 10minutes and above.

- For Victory and Abundant Blessings in all life s situations

I WILL LIKE YOU TO TAKE NOTES OF THE FOLLOWING.
1. Decide to serve your God with all your heart and might.
2. Decide to improve daily work with God.
3. Be a true tither, give offerings faithfully.
4. Meet the needs of the neediest, widows, orphans, disables and poor people.
5. Always live holy, praise foul and worshipful life.

Vow to give to God to draw His attention either in this ministry or any ministry you are lead to.

For Victory and Abundant Blessings in all life's situations

HOW TO ADMINISTER A PERSONAL DELIVERANCE

Deliverance is not something you do once and forget it altogether. It is to be done repeatedly and at regular intervals until your joy is full. If everything seems mixed up for you, take these steps: Decide to be delivered and believe that God will deliver you. There are three principal weapons of warfare you can use when administering a personal deliverance i.e. the Word of God, the Name of Jesus and the Blood of Jesus Christ.

a. In the Blood: We have the redemption and even the forgiveness of sins – *Colosians1: 14*.
b. The Word of God: is the Sword of the Spirit – *Ephesians 6: 17*.
c. The name of Jesus: every knee should bow – *Philippians 2; 9-11*.

BIBLE PASSAGES TO READ:
Obadiah 17; John 8:32; Romans. 8:2; II Corinthians.3: 17; Isaiah. 9:4; Luke10: 19; Revelation. 12:11; I John 4:4.

SONGS FOR DELIVERANCE:
I plead the blood, the blood of Jesus...
O the blood of Jesus, O the blood of Jesus...
When I survey the wondrous Cross...

PRAYER & DELIVERANCE:
1. Begin to call the blood of Jesus over your house and immediate environment for about 3 minutes
2. Call Holy Ghost fire to surround the house and environment for about 3 minutes. Begin to send all the evil spirits in your vicinity to the Red Sea and bind them there in Jesus name.
3. Now, stand or sit properly, place your right or left finger on your navel, place the other hand on your mouth as if you are about to drink water and begin to drink the blood of Jesus. Say "I drink the blood of Jesus" for about 10 minutes. In the spirit, envision the blood of Jesus as it is

■ For Victory and Abundant Blessings in all life's situations

passing through your mouth into your gullet, your chest and stomach.

4. After this, begin to command all the evil spirits troubling you to get out and go into the sea. Use ample time to send them out one after the other. Call them by their names. Do it for at least 5 minutes. Do it again and do it the third time. Do not be afraid peradventure you are about vomiting. Pour it out, do not swallow it. If you are yawning or belching or releasing anal gas, it is an indication that evil spirits are going out of your body. Let them go out.

5. Drink the blood of Jesus for about 5 minutes again, place your hand on your mouth as if you are drinking with your palms from the tap. Put the other hand on your navel and vomit or belch if you feel like doing so. Release the gas if you feel like it. Do not be afraid, let them go out.

6. Begin to cancel all the evil covenants you have made, covenants you have entered into before or that was made with you through blood, word, cloth, candle and spiritual bath in the river and all others. Cancel all of them in the name of Jesus. Have you taken your cloth to herbalist before or have you been bathed in the river? Have you prayed or been prayed for with demonic candles before? Have incisions been made on you or things like that? Use the blood of Jesus to cancel every demonic thing you know in your life *(Colossians 2:4)*. If you fail to do that genuinely, deliverance will not happen.

7. Call the Holy Ghost fire to surround you and destroy every covenant, the spirit and the works of the devil in your life or in your house, command that all items buried or hung on the wall or blown into the air because of you be destroyed in Jesus name. Confess that all magic mirrors being used to spy your destiny be shattered in Jesus name.

8. Now, ask the Holy Spirit to fill your life. **Say "Holy Spirit, enter my heart".** Say this for about 3 minutes. Make confession that your bondage is broken. Sing it and give thanks to the Creator.

Believe that Jesus has set you free; stay clear of sinful practices and thoughts; be prayerful, study the Word of God daily, fellowship with other believers and praise God always. God bless you.

BEGINNING A RELATIONSHIP WITH JESUS CHRIST

1. **Know** God loves you not for what you do, but for who you are. He has a wonderful purpose for your life. He seeks to love and lead you from now on till eternity. He wants to bless your life and make it full and complete.
And I, the Son of Man, have come to seek and save those like him who are lost. Luke 19:10
Jesus told him, *"I am the way, the truth, and the life. No one can come to the Father except through me. John 14:6*

2. **Admit** to God that you have made mistakes and have sinned. You may have heard people say, "I'm only human--nobody's perfect." The Bible says the same thing: We are all sinners. We all do things that we know are wrong. And that's why we feel estranged from God; because God is holy and good, and we are not.
"For all have sinned; all fall short of God's glorious standard". Romans 3:23
"For the wages of sin is death, but the free gift of God is eternal life through Christ Jesus our Lord". Roman 6:23.

3. **Understand** that Jesus Christ, the son of God, is the only one that can bring you into a full relationship with God. His death on the cross was the necessary payment to cover the cost of your sins and He did it for you.
But God showed his great love for us by sending Christ to die for us while we were still sinners. Roman 5:8
But if we confess our sins to him, he is faithful and just to forgive us and to cleanse us from every wrong. 1 John1:9

4. **Declare** Pray to God right now and sincerely seek forgiveness for your sins. Tell God you're sorry and ask Jesus Christ to be the saviour of your past and the Lord of your present and future.

For if you confess with your mouth that Jesus is Lord and believe in your heart that God raised him from the dead, you will be saved. Romans 10:9

PRAYER TO RECEIVE JESUS:

Lord Jesus, I need You. Thank you for dying on the cross for my sins. I open the door of my life and receive You as my Saviour and Lord. Thank you for forgiving my sins and giving me eternal life. Take control of the throne of my life. Make me into the kind of person you want me to be. In Jesus name I pray, Amen.

Celebrate as you stand as a new person in the eyes of God. The old sin and shame are gone and you are ready to discover your purpose in this life. Begin to walk with God daily by reading the bible and fellowshipping with other believers. Let the Spirit of God work in and through you as you begin this new life.

"In the same way, there is joy in the presence of God's angels when even one sinner repents." Luke 15:10

What this means is that those who become Christians become new persons. They are not the same anymore, for the old life is gone. A new life has begun! *2 Corinthians 5:17 (KJV)*

Welcome to the family of God. Start reading the Bible beginning with the gospel of John.

SCRIPTURE GUIDE

Some useful passages of the Bible for various situations and circumstances are listed below:

1 *YOU NEED SALVATION:*
   John.3: 1-21; Romans. 1:6-17; Romans.3: 21-31; Romans.5: 1-11; Romans. 10:5-13; Ephesians. 2:1-10.

2. *SEEKING FOR TRUTH:*
   Psalm.119:153-160; John.8: 31-47; 14:6-14; 16:14b, 15, 1Timothy.2: 1-7.

3. *YOU ARE CONFUSED:*
   Isaiah 51:11; Philippians.4: 6-8; Psalm.138: 7; John.14: 27; 2Corinthians. 4:8-9; Phiippiansl.1: 6; Psalm.31: 24; 27.

4. *THERE IS NO HELPER:*
   Hebrews 13:5, I Samuel. 12:2, Isaiah 41:10; John.14: 18; Deuteronoromy.33: 27; 4:31; 31:6; Psalm.5; 57; 86; 121; 130; 119:169-176.

5. *YOU HAVE NO JOY:*
   1Peter. 5:7; Jn.14: 1; Colossians.3: 15; Isaiah. 26:3; Proverbs.3: 24; Hebrews.4: 3; 9; Psalms. 119:165; John.14: 27; Philippians. 4:4

6. *YOU LACK CONTENTMENT:*
   Psalms 34: 10, Isaiah. 44:3; Psalm.37: 3; 63:1-5; Proverbs.12: 14; Jeremiah. 31:14; Psalm107: 9.

7. *YOU ARE CONFUSED:*
   1Corinthians. 14:33; II Timothy.1: 7; Isaiah.50: 7; Psalm.32: 8; James.1: 5; 1 Pet.er4: 12-13; Isaiah. 30:21, 43:2.

8. *YOU ARE IN TEMPTATION:*
   2 Corinthians. 10:12-13; Hebrews.4: 14-16, 2:18; 2 Peter. 2:9; James.1: 13-14; 1 Peter.5: 8-9; 1 John. 4:4; John.1: 2, 3, 12; 2 Peter.1:6-7.

9. *WHEN YOU NEED SOMEBODY TO TRUST*
   Psalm 27:14; Romans.8: 38-39; Psalm.118: 17; Isaiah.41: 10; Psalm.31: 24; Isaiah.43: 2-5.

For Victory and Abundant Blessings in all life's situations

10. **YOU NEED PEACE:**
Isaiah.55:12; Ps.37:37; Isaiah. 57:2; Romans.14: 17-19;
2 Cor.13: 11.

11. **YOU WANT TO MAKE A POWERFUL DECISION:**
1 King.3; Esther.4-7; Psalms.139; Daniel.2: 14-23;
Colosians.3: 14-17.

12. **YOU ARE SEEKING ADMISSION INTO SCHOOL:**
Proverbs.2: 1-8; 3:1-18; 4:1-27; 23:12; Romans.8: 1-17; 2
Corinthians. 1:18-31.

13. **YOU ARE STARTING A NEW JOB:**
Proverbs 11:3; 22:29; Romans.12: 3-11; 2 Thessalonians.5: 12-18;1
Peter. 4:7-11.

14. **YOU HAVE A CASE IN COURT:**
Psalms.26; Isaiah.50: 4-11; Matthew.5: 25; Luke.18: 1-8.

15. **YOU ARE ADDICTED TO SOMETHING:**
Psalms.40:1-5; 11-17; Psalms116:1-7; Proverbs.23:29-35;
11Corinthians.5: 16-21; Ephesians. 4:22-24.

16. **SEEKING FOR FORGIVENESS:**
Psalms. 32:1-5; Proverbs.28: 13; Joel 2:12-17; Matthew.6: 14-15;
Luke. 15; Philemon; Hebrews.4: 14-16; 1John.1: 5-10.

17. **YOU ARE SAD:**
I Thesalonians.4: 13-14; II Thessalonians.2: 16-18; 1 Corinthians1:
3-6; Isaiah.61: 1-3; Psalm.23: 4; Hebrews.4:15-16; Revelation 21: 4.

18. **YOU ARE IN DOUBT:**
Mark.11: 17-24; Luke.12: 29-31; Romans.4: 20-21; Isaiah.46:10-
11; 1 Thess.5: 24; 2 Pet.3: 9; Isaiah 59:1; 55:10-11.

19. **YOU ARE LOOKING UNTO GOD FOR HELP:**
Psalm 27: 14; 62:5; Hebrews.2: 3; Psalms.10: 5.

20. **YOU ARE FACED WITH DISAPPOINTMENT AND REJECTION FROM A LOVED ONE:**
Psalms 9:10; 94:14; 27:10; 91:14-15; 2 Corinthians.4: 9; I Peter.5: 7;
Isa.41: 17; 2 Samuel12: 22.

21. **YOU DO NOT UNDERSTAND THE WAYS OF GOD:**
Jeremiah 33:3; 1 Corinthians.10: 13; Psalm.138: 8; Romans.8: 23.

22. YOU ARE IN OLD AGE:
Isaiah.46: 4; Psalm.77: 17-18; Proverbs.20: 21; 16:31; Psalms.92: 14; Psalm.37: 23-29; 23:4; Isaiah.46: 3-4; Matthew.28: 20.

23. YOU ARE SICK:
III John.2; Matthew.9: 35; 2 Peter.2: 24; Jeremiah.17: 14; 30:17; Exodus.15: 26; Proverbs.4: 20-22; James.5: 14-15; Mark.16: 17-18; Psalms.6: 1-10.

24. YOU ARE AFRAID OF THE WICKED:
Psalms. 27; 91; Isaiah.41: 5-13; Mark.4: 35-41; Hebrews.13: 5-6; I John.4: 13-18.

25. YOU ARE AFRAID OF DEATH:
Psalms.23; 63: 1-8; Romans.8: 18-39; 1 Corinthians.15: 35-57; 2 Corianthians.5: 1-10; 2 Timothy.1: 8-10.

26. THE SPIRIT OF FORNICATION OR ADULTERY IS ABOUT RESTING ON YOU:
2 Samuel.11: 7-12, 25; I Corinthians. 6:12-20; Galatians. 5:16-2

27. YOU WANT TO TAKE REVENGE:
Matthew.5: 36-42; Romans.12: 17-21

28. SPIRIT OF JEALOUSY IS TROUBLING YOU:
Psalms. 49; Proverbs.23: 17; James.3: 13-18.

29. YOU ARE RETIRING:
Numbers.6: 24-26; Psalms145; Matthew.25: 31-46; Romans.12: 1-12; Philippians.3: 3; 12:21; 2Pet.1-2.

30. YOU ARE AFRAID OF THE FUTURE:
Isaiah. 35:60; Jeremiah.29: 10-14; I Peter.1: 3-5; Revelation.21: 1-8.

For Victory and Abundant Blessings in all life's situations

PROGRAMS AND EVENTS
CHRIST TOTAL GOSPEL MINISTRIES
INTERNATIONAL (CHRTOGM)

1. ANNUALLY
REVIVAL OF HIS CHURCH
- Every second week of November in Abeokuta.
- Every third week of July in Kaduna
- Every last week of October in Lagos
- Every third week of October in London

2. MONTHLY
JESUS NIGHT OF DELIVERANCE
- *Time: Every 3rd Friday of the month 10.00PM*
  Venue: (Abeokuta) All Nations for Christ Baptist Church,
  Ita-iyalode. Abeokuta

- *Time: Every third Thursday of the month. (6.00-9.00pm)*
  Venue: (UK) All Nations for Christ Baptist Church,   B e t t y
  Strathern Community Hall, 41 Myrtle Road Harold Hill, Romford,
  United Kingdom, RM3 8XS

- *Time: Quarterly every year*
  Venue: Lagos

- *Time: Four times a year*
  Venue: Ogbomosho and Ibadan

FROM GLORY TO GLORY
- *Time: Every 1st to 3rd day of each month*
  Venue: All Nations for Christ Baptist Church, Ita-iyalode Abeokuta
  5:30pm

| 151 |

For Victory and Abundant Blessings in all life's situations

3. WEEKLY
BUSINESS PEOPLE PRAYER MEETING
Time: Every Monday at 6:30 am
Venue: All Nations for Christ Baptist Church, Abeokuta

ORO MI O YANJU
Time: (Bi-weekly) Every other Thursdays
Venue: All Nations for Christ Baptist Church, Ita-iyalode Abeokuta

ORO MI O YANJU TV AND RADIO OUTREACH
Time: Sundays 7:00pm

INTERNET:
TELEPHONE MIDNIGHT PRAYER CONFERENCE MEETING
SUNDAY'S 12.00 MIDNIGHTS

CHURCH BULLETIN
Revival of His Church Bulletin

BOOKS BY
PETER O. ADENMOSUN

1. *Divine Healing for your Marriage*
2. *Dilemma and Redemption of the Firstborns*
3. *You and Your Dreams*
4. *Procrastination and the way out*
5. *Deliverance from Bondages*
6. *New Breakthrough Prayers (6 editions)*
7. *The Blood of Jesus, Our Ground for Total Victory*
8. *Be Wise Win Souls*
9. *Biblical Confessional Prayers*
10. *Winning Your World (Soul Winning At Its Best)*
11. *The Church And Information Technology*
12. *Adura Agbayori Titun (Yoruba)*
13. *Iwo ati Ala Re (Yoruba)*

For Victory and Abundant Blessings in all life's situations

PARTNERSHIP FORM

We will appreciate it if you can partner with us in this ministry.

I wish to participate in this ministry (Tick any of the options) as you prayerfully wish

* **As Prayer partner** *(I Thessalonians 3:1-3)*
* **As Volunteer Worker** *(I Corinthians 3)*
* **By Seed Faith Partner** *(I Corinthians 13:9)*

☐ *Quayrterly*   ☐ *Monthly*   ☐ *Annually*

Name ....

Address ....

Phone ....

E-mail ....

Your Prayer Requests or Suggestion.

- For Victory and Abundant Blessings in all life s situations

New Breakthrough Prayers

For Victory and Abundant Blessings in all life s situations